THE OFFICIAL
LIVERPOOL FC
BOOK OF RECORDS

A CIP catalogue record for this book is
available from the British Library

Carlton Books Limited
20 Mortimer Street
London W1T 3JW

ISBN: 978-1-78097-337-1

Editor: Martin Corteel
Art Director: Darren Jordan
Design: emc Design Limited
Picture Research: Paul Langan
Production: Rachel Burgess

Printed in Dubai

THE OFFICIAL
LIVERPOOL FC
BOOK OF RECORDS

JEFF ANDERSON

CARLTON
BOOKS

Contents

BELOW (from left to right): Steven Gerrard lifts the Champions League trophy in 2005; the Reds' league championship-winning side in 1989–90; Ian Callaghan – Liverpool's longest-serving player; Bill Shankly – the manager who started the Reds' revolution; Jamie Carragher – the club's longest-serving player of modern times; celebrating FA Cup success over Arsenal in 2001

Introduction

In the beginning there was a stadium but no team. In 1892 Anfield's occupants, Everton FC, quit in a dispute over rent, leaving their landlord and former chairman with an empty ground. John Houlding could have sold the land off, cashed in his profit, and withdrawn from football to concentrate on his burgeoning business and political interests. Instead, the brewer, philanthropist and future Lord Mayor of Liverpool set about founding an entirely new club, which he named after his home city.

Within a year Liverpool were members of the Football League and, by the turn of the century, were serious rivals to the team that Houlding had previously bankrolled and developed. In the years that followed they would not only usurp Everton as the main football force on Merseyside; they would go on to dominate the game in England, sweep all before them in Europe and win the support and loyalty of millions of fans around the world.

With 18 League titles, 15 domestic Cups, plus a dazzling array of other team and individual awards, Liverpool are among the most successful clubs in the history of the English game. In top-flight football no other team has won as many matches, or amassed as many points. In Europe, their 11 finals and eight major trophies put them in a class of their own when it comes to competing for honours abroad.

Yet, while LFC may be 'all about winning things' – as a former chairman once said – the silverware is only part of what makes the club special. Over the last 121 years there have been tragedies as well as triumphs, lean years to go alongside the trophy-laden seasons. Legendary players have performed astonishing personal feats. Charismatic managers have built and motivated teams that have scaled new heights. And along the way, a world-famous crowd has inspired unlikely victories and epic fight-backs.

Not everyone can make it into the record books, but all of the above deserve their place. This book celebrates their achievements and their contributions to the story of a unique football club.

BELOW: Anfield's Kop in full cry as Liverpool warm up for the Premier League match against Chelsea in April 2013

Liverpool Team Records

When Liverpool beat Aston Villa in March 2013 they became the first English club to record 1,800 wins in top-flight football. Those victories, notched up during 110 seasons in the First Division and Premier League, also helped them amass more points than any of their rivals.

The following table takes into account all results since the inaugural Football League in 1888 – four years prior to Liverpool's formation, and six years before their first top-flight appearance. It awards two points for a win and one for a draw up to the end of the 1980-81 campaign, and three points for a win, plus one for a draw, in subsequent seasons.

ALL-TIME TOP-FLIGHT POINTS TABLE

Rank	Club	Points
1	Liverpool	5,231
2	Arsenal	5,173
3	Everton	5,063
4	Manchester United	4,984
5	Aston Villa	4,619
6	Chelsea	3,854

UP FOR THE CUPS

When it comes to knockout competitions, Liverpool are also out in front. Domestically, they have won eight League and seven FA Cups – a joint record. On the continent, their three UEFA Cup final victories are unsurpassed. They have won the Super Cup more times than any other British team. And, in 2005, they became only the third club to keep the European Cup permanently: the result of winning the trophy on five separate occasions.

DOMESTIC CUPS

Rank	Club	Trophies
1	Liverpool	15 (8 LC, 7 FAC)
2	Manchester United	15 (4 LC, 11 FAC)
3	Aston Villa	12 (5 LC, 7 FAC)
4	Tottenham Hotspur	12 (4 LC, 8 FAC)
5	Arsenal	12 (2 LC, 10 FAC)
6	Chelsea	11 (4 LC, 7 FAC)

EUROPEAN CUPS (ENGLISH CLUBS ONLY)

Rank	Club	Trophies
1	Liverpool	11 (5 EC, 3 UEFA, 3 SC)
2	Manchester United	5 (3 EC, 1 CWC, 1 SC)
3	Chelsea	5 (1 EC, 2 CWC, 1 Europa, 1 SC)
4	Nottingham Forest	3 (2 EC, 1 SC)
5	Tottenham Hotspur	3 (2 UEFA, 1 CWC)

ABOVE: Captain Steven Gerrard celebrates after scoring Liverpool's second goal in a 2–1 defeat of Aston Villa at Villa Park in March 2013

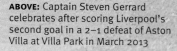

Football League Records

Up to the introduction of the Premier League Liverpool dominated the Football League Championship, topping the First Division table in 18 different seasons. Their nearest rivals, Arsenal and Everton, were way behind with 10 and nine titles apiece.

Although success didn't come instantly for the so-called 'Anfielders', they did reach the summit of the English game less than a decade after being formed. Five years later they were Champions again, becoming the first club to clinch promotion, then the title, in successive seasons. There were further periods of success, both in the early 1920s and immediately after World War II. But it wasn't until the 1960s, with Bill Shankly at the helm, that the Reds began to reach their full potential.

This section highlights the records Liverpool set from their earliest days in the Second Division to their era of unprecedented League success.

ABOVE: Pot 'n' boots. Paisley in the Anfield 'boot room' with one of his six League title trophies

OPPOSITE: Bob Paisley holds the 1983 League Championship aloft before his last home game as manager

 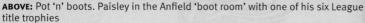

Biggest Wins

▶▶ NINE FROM EIGHT

Only once in Liverpool's history have eight different players got on the scoresheet in a single League match. It happened on 12 September 1989 when Kenny Dalglish's team thrashed Crystal Palace 9–0 in one of the finest performances Anfield has ever witnessed.

Steve Nicol began the rout in the seventh minute, with Steve McMahon and Ian Rush both netting before the interval. Centre-back Gary Gillespie nodded home a fourth, then Peter Beardsley added a fifth before making way for John Aldridge who scored from the penalty spot with his first touch. John Barnes and Glenn Hysen both added goals before Nicol – the man who started it all – finished Palace off with a ninth just two minutes from time.

ANFIELD IN SEVENTH HEAVEN

Liverpool have won three home League games 7–0. The first was in 1902 when Stoke City, ravaged by food poisoning, could only field a team of nine men. Several of those who did make it onto the pitch had to leave during the match to pay emergency visits to the gents' toilets, and at one stage there were only seven of them remaining. Reds' striker Andy McGuigan took full advantage, hitting the target five times – the first Liverpool player to do so. It would be another 52 years before that feat was repeated.

LEFT: Ray Houghton put the seventh goal past Derby County in March 1991

RIGHT: Reds' 'Mr Versatile' Steve Nicol was on target twice in the 9–0 annihilation of Crystal Palace

BIGGEST HOME WINS – FOOTBALL LEAGUE

10–1	v	Rotherham Town, Division Two, 18 February 1896
9–0	v	Crystal Palace, Division One, 12 September 1989
8–0	v	Burnley, Division One, 26 December 1928
9–2	v	Grimsby Town, Division One, 6 December 1902
8–1	v	Burslem Port Vale, Division Two, 8 April 1905

◀◀ SHAME FOR SHILTON

The 7–1 win at the Baseball Ground in March 1991 remains Liverpool's biggest-ever away victory in the top flight. The achievement was all the more special as Derby County's goalkeeper that day was Peter Shilton, England's most capped player of all-time. He picked the ball out the net after efforts from John Barnes and Steve Nicol – who grabbed two apiece – and Jan Molby, Ian Rush and Ray Houghton.

COULD HAVE BEEN MORE

The Reds' 8–0 Boxing Day win against Burnley in 1928 stood as their record top-flight victory for nearly 61 years. But, had it not been for bad luck and some questionable decisions, the margin might have been much greater. Liverpool had three goals disallowed, hit the woodwork at least four times, and even managed to miss a penalty.

STORY OF THE BLUES

The biggest home and away victories both came during the last season in which Liverpool played in their original colours. They had inherited the blue-and-white quarter shirts from Everton in 1892, keeping them for four years. But on 1 September 1896 they began the new First Division campaign with a visit to 'The Wednesday' where, for the first time, they sported white shorts and red shirts 'with a dark red or black stand collar with buttons down the front'.

HIGHEST AWAY WINS – FOOTBALL LEAGUE

7–0	v	Burton Swifts, Division Two, 29 February 1896
7–0	v	Crewe Alexandra, Division Two, 28 March 1896
7–1	v	Derby County, Division One, 23 March 1991
6–0	v	Wolves, Division One, 28 September 1968
6–1	v	Grimsby Town, Division One, 5 October 1946
6–1	v	Coventry City, Division One, 5 May 1990

LEFT: Hat-trick hero. John Barnes scored three of the Reds' six goals against Coventry in May 1990

IT'S A RECORD, BY GEORGE!

Liverpool's record League win was on 18 February 1896, as they pushed for promotion from Division Two. 'Inclement weather' for the match against Rotherham Town reduced the Anfield crowd to around 2,000 according to one newspaper of the time. And it seems those who did attend weren't impressed by the 10–1 victory. 'The general tone of the play, by virtue of Liverpool's immeasurable superiority, scarcely aroused a particle of enthusiasm,' the report added.

England striker Frank Becton got one of the goals, captain Jimmy Ross hit two, and inside-forward Malcolm McVean weighed in with a hat-trick. But the star of the afternoon was George 'Dod' Allan who, for the second time that season, was on target four times in a single match. Allan finished the campaign with a remarkable 25 goals in only 20 League appearances. In April 1897, a year after helping the club secure their place in Division One, he became the first Liverpool player to be capped by Scotland.

MALCOLM IN THE MIDDLE

As well as netting three in the 10–1 win over Rotherham Town, Malcolm McVean also played a major part in three other landmark victories. He scored twice in an 8–0 win over Higher Walton in September 1892, the club's biggest in the Lancashire League. The following month he bagged another brace as his team chalked up a record-breaking 9–0 FA Cup victory over Newtown. And in March 1896 his two goals helped Liverpool to a 7–0 win at Crewe Alexandra – still their joint best away result in the League.

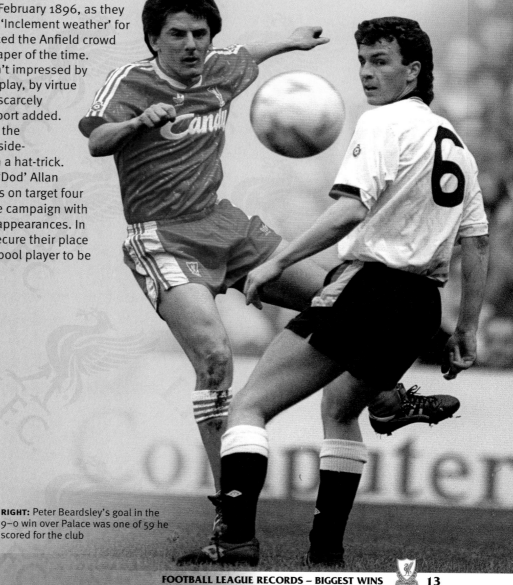

RIGHT: Peter Beardsley's goal in the 9–0 win over Palace was one of 59 he scored for the club

Biggest Defeats

TROUBLE WITH THE NEIGHBOURS

Between 1899 and 1920 Everton were unbeaten at Anfield, notching up 10 victories and six draws. Liverpool's low point during that most miserable of runs came on 3 October 1914, when the Blues crossed the park to deliver a 5–0 thrashing. To this day, it remains Liverpool's worst defeat in the Merseyside derby.

▼ FEELING GLUM IN BRUM

Reds fans who'd seen their side lose 8–0 to Huddersfield Town back in 1934 thought they would never witness anything as bad. But then came the visit to Birmingham City on a freezing afternoon two decades later, and an even worse humiliation.

Boss Don Welsh took his players to St Andrews on 11 December 1954, shortly after telling reporters he was determined to win promotion back to Division One at the first attempt. But this match shattered his illusions. His side capitulated, falling a goal behind after just 48 seconds, trailing 4–1 at the interval, and eventually suffering a miserable 9–1 defeat.

The 17,500 crowd could barely believe what was happening, and neither, it seemed, did the visiting team.

'It was the middle of winter, the pitch was frozen, it was hard underneath and wet on top,' recalled left-winger Alan A'Court many years later. 'We were slipping and sliding all over the place and went three goals down in the first 15 minutes. Billy Liddell pulled one back for us and I still say that was the best of the ten! He kept his balance beautifully on that surface, turned like an ice-skater and hit a screamer into the top corner of the net. It was a one-off game. I cannot explain why it happened. The game kept slipping away, literally.'

LEFT: Alan A'Court was in the line-up for the 9–1 drubbing at St. Andrews – but probably wished he wasn't

BIGGEST HOME DEFEATS – FOOTBALL LEAGUE

0–6	v Sunderland, Division One, 19 April 1930
1–6	v Manchester City, Division One, 26 October 1929
0–5	v Everton, Division One, 3 October 1914
0–5	v Manchester City, Division One, 26 March 1937
1–5	v Newcastle United, Division One, 14 December 1907
1–5	v Wolves, Division One, 7 December 1946
1–5	v Arsenal, Division One, 15 November 1952
1–5	v Preston North End, Division One, 5 September 1953

A SEASON TO FORGET

In the 1953–54 season the Reds recorded their highest number of defeats in any single campaign, losing 23 of their 42 matches. Their worst home result was a 5–1 reverse against Preston North End. While on the road they lost 6–0 at Charlton, 5–1 at Portsmouth and Manchester United, and 5–2 at West Bromwich Albion.

Although the team were relegated with just 28 points, they did manage to score 68 times in the League – 17 more than Cardiff City who finished in 10th place. But their terrible defensive frailties meant they shipped an incredible 97 goals in the League – the most the team has ever conceded in one season.

BOBBY DAZZLER

Sunderland are responsible for inflicting Liverpool's heaviest home defeat, hitting six goals without reply in April 1930. Four of them came from the club's all-time highest scorer Bobby Gurney. Eight months later, when the two teams met at Roker Park, Gurney grabbed a hat-trick as the Reds went down 6–5.

▼ BAD START FOR ARTHUR

Liverpool's worst opening day defeat was in August 1937 when they lost 6–1 to Chelsea at Stamford Bridge. The second heaviest loss was eight years earlier when they went down 5–0 to Middlesbrough at Ayresome Park. South African born keeper Arthur Riley was between the posts on both occasions.

▶▶ ELISHA ON THE RECEIVING END

All of Liverpool's five heaviest defeats have been in League matches away from Anfield – three of them in 1934. On 1 January, Elisha Scott was in goal against Newcastle, exactly 21 years after making his Liverpool debut. But it was an unhappy anniversary for the keeper as he conceded nine times – more than in any match during his long and illustrious career.

E. SCOTT
LIVERPOOL

ABOVE: Elisha Scott – between the sticks for the 9–2 defeat at Newcastle

BELOW: Strife of Riley. Arthur (standing in the middle of the back row) had two nightmare starts to the season

BIGGEST AWAY DEFEATS – FOOTBALL LEAGUE

1–9 v Birmingham City, Division Two, 11 December 1954	
0–8 v Huddersfield Town, Division One, 10 November 1934	
2–9 v Newcastle United, Division One, 1 January 1934	
1–8 v Bolton Wanderers, Division One, 7 May 1932	
1–8 v Arsenal, Division One, 1 September 1934	

Winning Sequences

▶▶ BOB'S LAST FLING

In Bob Paisley's final season as manager, Liverpool recorded a sequence of nine straight wins, then a second run of 10. Only a short dip in form, which included one defeat and a draw in December 1982, prevented the Reds from shattering all previous records.

The second winning spell, starting on New Year's Day 1983, and ending almost six weeks later, left the Reds 15 points clear at the top of the table. They effectively sealed the Championship with a 3–0 win over Swansea at Anfield in April. It was all downhill afterwards, though. With the title already in the bag, they played seven more games, drawing two and losing five.

▼ FINISHING WITH A FLOURISH

The League and FA Cup double in Kenny Dalglish's first season as player-manager came on the back of nine straight wins in both competitions. Before the winning streak began at the end of March 1986, Liverpool were two points behind Everton at the top of the table, and still had to overcome Southampton in the semi-final of the Cup.

But the Reds proved to be imperious during the run-in, sweeping the Saints aside, and getting maximum points from their last seven League matches. The last of those was at Stamford Bridge where a goal from Dalglish himself secured the title. One week later, the team completed their run with a 3–1 win over Everton at Wembley.

ABOVE: Fond farewell. Bob Paisley clinched the title with seven games remaining

BELOW: Thanks boss. Kenny Dalglish was the goalscoring hero as Liverpool beat Chelsea on the final day of the season to win the league title in 1985–86

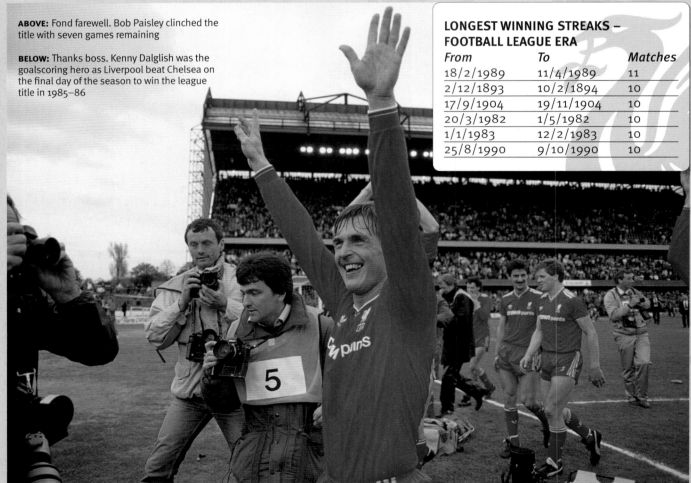

LONGEST WINNING STREAKS – FOOTBALL LEAGUE ERA

From	To	Matches
18/2/1989	11/4/1989	11
2/12/1893	10/2/1894	10
17/9/1904	19/11/1904	10
20/3/1982	1/5/1982	10
1/1/1983	12/2/1983	10
25/8/1990	9/10/1990	10

HOT STREAK

Liverpool's longest winning streak in the Football League era was in the 1988–89 season when Kenny Dalglish guided his men to victory in nine First Division matches and two FA Cup ties. At the end of the surge, Liverpool were top of the League on goal difference, but they eventually lost the title to Arsenal. Consolation came in the form of their fourth FA Cup thanks to a 3–2 defeat of Everton.

SEASON OF VICTORY

Although the Reds never put together a record-breaking run of victories in the 1978–79 season, they did win more matches than in any other campaign. Bob Paisley's men took maximum points from 30 of their 42 games, drawing eight and losing only four. They also finished with 85 goals, an average of more than two each match.

For most fans, the highlight was the 7–0 demolition of Tottenham in September 1978. The seventh – a header from Terry McDermott who ran the entire length of the pitch to finish a sweeping box-to-box move – is still widely considered to be the finest goal ever scored at Anfield.

STARTER FOR TEN

Liverpool's 10 successive wins between August and October 1990 gave them their best ever start to a First Division season. Aside from two League Cup victories, the Reds chalked up maximum points from their opening eight First Division fixtures. Highlights included a 4–0 thrashing of Manchester United at Anfield, and a 3–2 win at Goodison in the Merseyside derby. After such a blistering start, most people thought the team were on their way to a 19th title. But their challenge faded as the campaign went on, and Arsenal – who lost just one game all season – finished seven points clear at the top.

KENNY'S KILLER RUN

Date	Opposition	Result	Competition
18/2/1989	Hull City (a)	3–2	FA Cup Fifth Round
1/3/1989	Charlton Athletic (h)	2–0	Division One
11/3/1989	Middlesbrough (a)	4–0	Division One
14/3/1989	Luton Town (h)	5–0	Division One
18/3/1989	Brentford (h)	4–0	FA Cup Sixth Round
22/3/1989	Coventry City (a)	3–1	Division One
26/3/1989	Tottenham Hotspur (a)	2–1	Division One
29/3/1989	Derby County (h)	1–0	Division One
1/4/1989	Norwich City (a)	1–0	Division One
8/4/1989	Sheffield Wednesday (h)	5–1	Division One
11/4/1989	Millwall (a)	2–1	Division One

▼ ANFIELD'S FIRST FULL HOUSE

The club's first run of 10 straight wins in all competitions took place in the 1893–94 season. The final victory came in the team's biggest match up to that period: an FA Cup Second Round home tie against Preston North End. So great was the excitement surrounding the visit of the so-called 'Invincibles' that Anfield experienced its first-ever lock-out, with hordes of fans being turned away. The 18,000 who did manage to get in witnessed a pulsating tie in which Liverpool grabbed a late winner after throwing away an early two-goal lead. Sadly, they lost to Bolton in the next round, bringing their run, and their FA Cup hopes, to an end.

BELOW: Terry McDermott celebrates after his sensational headed goal against Spurs in September 1978

Undefeated Records

▼ THE OTHER KING KENNY

Liverpool went on a 15-match unbeaten run at Anfield in the back half of the 1919–20 season, setting a new record for consecutive clean sheets along the way. Between January and April, the Reds didn't concede a single goal in home League and Cup matches – a feat that wouldn't be repeated for another 86 years.

Glaswegian keeper Kenny Campbell was responsible for eight of the 10 shut-outs, in a season when he re-established himself in the side due to Elisha Scott's unavailability. The Scottish international, whose good looks made him one of football's early pin-ups, was a regular before World War I, and part of the 1914 FA Cup final line-up. His post-war form helped Liverpool to a top-five finish. But, as soon as Scott returned from loan spells in Ireland, it was time for Campbell to make way once more.

LEFT: 'Mr. Clean'. Kenny Campbell helped shut out the opposition in the 1919–20 season

BELOW: Class of '87–88. Dalglish's 'great entertainers' were unbeaten in their opening 29 games

▼ BAD DAY AT GOODISON

The team assembled by Kenny Dalglish for the 1987–88 season is generally considered to be one of the best in Liverpool's history, and certainly the most entertaining. They finished as Champions, nine points ahead of their closest rivals, and with 26 wins to their credit. Dalglish's irresistible side went unbeaten in their first 29 League games. But their run came to an abrupt end at Goodison Park on 20 March 1988, when a single Wayne Clarke goal gave Everton victory in the Merseyside derby. It was only Liverpool's second defeat in all competitions up to that point in the season – and, again, Everton were the team responsible, knocking their neighbours out of the League Cup in a Third Round tie at Anfield.

Liverpool lost just two more matches during that whole campaign: away to Nottingham Forest in the League, and against Wimbledon in the FA Cup final at Wembley.

ABOVE: Liverpool Football Club in 1893–94

RIGHT: The famous sign which some players touch for luck as they run onto the Anfield pitch

▲ ANFIELD'S INVINCIBLES

Exactly a century before Arsenal went through an entire Premiership campaign unbeaten, Liverpool fielded its own team of 'Invincibles'. In 1893–94, the club's first season in the Football League, they won 22 of their 28 Second Division matches, drawing six and losing none.

The team collected maximum points from every home League fixture that season – another club record that's still to be equalled. They hit 77 goals, and failed to score just once. In defence they were just as impressive, conceding only 18 goals, and recording 14 shut-outs.

Unsurprisingly, Liverpool finished eight points ahead of their nearest rivals. But promotion still rested on the outcome of a 'Test Match', an early form of play-off between the top club in Division Two and the bottom team in Division One. That took place at Ewood Park, Blackburn, on 28 April 1894, when Liverpool beat Newton Heath – later to be renamed Manchester United – by two goals to nil.

ONE RUN, TWO SEASONS

The longest unbeaten run in all competitions came in 1982. Between March and September that year, Liverpool played in 25 League, Charity Shield and European games without loss.

The sequence began after a 0–2 defeat away to CSKA Sofia in the European Cup. With nothing other than the League to focus on, Liverpool then won 12 and drew three of their last 15 First Division games, to take the title comfortably. They then started the following campaign exactly as they had left off, first beating Tottenham in the Shield clash at Wembley, then winning five League matches and drawing two others. It was only after winning the second of their European Cup matches against Dundalk that the bandwagon finally stopped rolling. The Reds visited Ipswich Town, where an 81st minute goal gave the home side victory.

▲ THE IMPREGNABLE FORTRESS

Bill Shankly said he put up the 'This Is Anfield' sign to frighten other teams as they walked through the tunnel. But it was during Bob Paisley's reign that the opposition was most scared. In the three years between January 1978 and January 1981 his Reds side never lost a single home game.

The 85-match sequence included games in the League and domestic and European cup competitions. Full-back Phil Neal, who holds the record for most consecutive LFC appearances, played in all of them.

The amazing run came to an end on 31 January 1981, when Leicester City – a traditional bogey side – earned themselves a 2–1 win. The result was all the more surprising as Leicester were then second from bottom of the table – and were later relegated.

League Championship Winners

◄◄ **THANKS TO THE YANKS**

In the summer of 1946 the Anfield board decided to bypass post-war food rationing by taking the team on a pre-season tour of North America. As a result of their month-long diet of steak and other luxuries, the players came back to Britain an average of 10lb heavier. Their newfound bulk certainly didn't do them any harm, as they finished the season at the top of the table, thanks largely to strikers Albert Stubbins and Jack Balmer both 'weighing in' with 24 League goals.

However, a severe winter had caused many fixtures to be postponed and Liverpool had to wait until 14 June 1947, to see if their nearest rivals Stoke City could win their final match to overtake them. In the event, they couldn't. As the Potters went down to Sheffield United, the Reds were beating Everton in a Liverpool Senior Cup final in front of 40,000 fans at Anfield. As the result from Bramall Lane was announced over the public address system, players and fans were able to celebrate winning two trophies in one day.

ABOVE: George Kay (back row, left), took the Reds to the USA for preseason in 1946 and Liverpool ended 1946–47 as Champions

PAISLEY'S PRIDE

Paisley's last Championship success in 1983 made him the first manager to deliver six League titles since Aston Villa boss George Ramsay more than seven decades earlier.

Of all those titles, none was won with such style and ease as in the 1978–79 season. His team won 30 of their 42 matches, drawing eight, losing just four, and finishing the campaign with an astonishing goal difference of 69. Their points tally of 68 was the all-time club record under the old two-points-for-a-win system.

THE FIRST HOMECOMING

Liverpool clinched their first-ever League title with a 1–0 win over West Brom at the Hawthorns on the final day of the 1900–01 season. Amazingly, it was the first time they had topped the table since the opening day of the campaign.

The players and directors returned to the city's Central Station late that Monday evening to be greeted by thousands of fans, plus a drum and fife band playing 'The Conquering Hero'. Among those to be carried shoulder-high through the streets were captain Alex Raisbeck and leading marksman Sam Raybould – who would later become the first Liverpool striker to hit 100 League goals.

BACK-TO-BACK TITLES

In 1923 Liverpool lifted the Championship for the second year running – equalling the achievements of Preston North End, Sunderland, Aston Villa and Sheffield Wednesday. It would be another 54 years before the Reds could celebrate their next back-to-back title success.

BELOW: Familiar faces. The names on the Reds team-sheet rarely changed during the 1965–66 season

THE OLD ONE TWO

The Reds won their 1905–06 title just 12 months after being promoted as Second Division Champions. Only three other clubs have since managed to top the Division Two and One tables in successive seasons: Everton (1931–32), Tottenham (1950–51) and Ipswich (1961–62)

LEAGUE TITLES – LEAST PLAYERS USED

1965–66:	14
1978–79:	15
1983–84:	15
1972–73:	16
1981–82:	16
1982–83:	16

DREAM DEBUT SEASONS

In 1984 Joe Fagan became the first Liverpool manager to win the League title in his debut campaign – an achievement matched by Kenny Dalglish two years later. Both men added other trophies to their first-season haul. Fagan landed both the European and League Cups, while Dalglish completed the club's only League–FA Cup double.

Dalglish's second Championship – in the 1987–88 season – was secured with 90 points from 40 games: a club record in the three-points-for-a-win era.

THE PAPER BOYS

Bill Shankly's team secured their first League title in style, beating Arsenal 5–0 on an unforgettable April Saturday in 1964. But their hopes of showing off the Championship trophy to delirious supporters were dashed when previous holders, Everton, insisted on returning it to the Football league instead. One enterprising fan wasn't to be outdone, however. He made a papier-mache version of the trophy, which skipper Ron Yeats duly paraded around the ground once the final whistle had gone.

BELOW: Ron Yeats and Willie Stevenson (left) parade the 'replica' trophy in April 1964

ABOVE: Kenny Dalglish with assistants Ronnie Moran and Roy Evans and the 1990 Championship trophy

CHAMPION OF CHAMPIONS

At the end of the 1975–76 season Bob Paisley landed his first title, and Liverpool overtook Arsenal as the most successful club in English League history. Five more titles from Paisley, one from Joe Fagan and three from Kenny Dalglish kept Liverpool at the top of the table of Championship-winners for another 35 years. However in 2011, Manchester United finally overtook them by landing their 19th title.

SHANKS' HAT-TRICK

Shankly's further League successes in 1966 and 1973 made him the first Reds boss to win the Championship three times. He delivered his second title using just 14 players – Liverpool's smallest-ever Championship-winning squad. The biggest squad was in 1946–47 when George Kay used a 26-strong pool of players to land his one and only title.

Premier League Records

Despite never winning the English Premier League, Liverpool have consistently been among the leading challengers, finishing in the top four on a dozen occasions and twice ending the season as runners-up.

At the end of the 2012–13 season they lie fourth in the all-time Premier League rankings with 1,3995 points from 810 games – 237 points ahead of fifth placed Tottenham Hotspur. They have also won 48.9% of those games, compared to 46.82 per cent of matches in the old First and Second Divisions.

ALL-TIME PREMIER LEAGUE TABLE*

Team	Points
Manchester United	1,752
Arsenal	1,522
Chelsea	1,477
Liverpool	1,395
Tottenham	1,158

*As at the end of 2012–13 season

BELOW: The Premier League trophy is a rare prize never to have visited Anfield

Biggest Wins

▶▶ TORRES TAKES AIM

Fernando Torres' Liverpool career was less than a month old when he helped them to their second biggest Premier League victory at Anfield. But his two goals in the 6–0 win over Derby County were soon to be eclipsed by many more breathtaking performances.

The Spaniard ended the 2007–08 campaign with 24 top-flight goals – more than any other Liverpool debutant since Albert Stubbins 61 years earlier. It was the biggest goals haul by any overseas player since the Premiership began. On his way to that final tally, Torres scored in eight home League matches, equalling a record set by sixties star, Roger Hunt.

AMAZING START, INCREDIBLE FINISH

Roy Evans delivered Liverpool's best opening day victory for 102 years, beating Crystal Palace 6–1 on their home turf on the first weekend of the 1994–95 season. Despite the flying start, his side were unable to mount a serious title challenge and ended the season in fourth place.

Still, the campaign ended even more memorably than it began. Liverpool beat Kenny Dalglish's Blackburn 2–1 on the last day, but – as Manchester United could only draw their fixture – Rovers actually clinched the Premiership title at Anfield.

SIX AND THE CITY

The Reds' 6–0 Premiership victory over Manchester City in 1995 came just three days after they met the Sky Blues in the League Cup at Anfield. The result of that Third Round tie? Liverpool 4 Man City 0.

RIGHT: Two from Torres. The striker helped crush Derby at Anfield in September 2007

BELOW: Luis Suarez's goal against Swansea was among 29 he scored in 2012–13

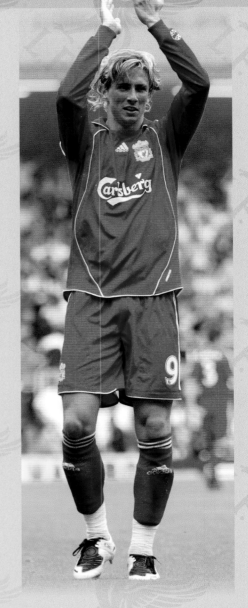

◀◀ FIVE STAR REDS

Liverpool have notched up eight 5–0 victories at Anfield since the Premier League began. The first was in November 1992 when two goals from Steve McManaman, plus further strikes from Mike Marsh, Ronny Rosenthal and Don Hutchinson, destroyed Crystal Palace. The last was in February 2013 when Steven Gerrard, Philippe Coutinho, Jose Enrique, Luis Suarez and Daniel Sturridge all combined to sink Swansea.

BIGGEST HOME WINS – PREMIER LEAGUE

7–1	v Southampton,	16 January 1999
6–0	v Derby County,	1 September 2007
6–0	v Manchester City,	28 October 1995
6–1	v Hull City,	26 September 2009

◀◀ VINTAGE DOUBLE ACT...

Robbie Fowler's second hat-trick of the 1998–99 season helped Liverpool achieve a 7–1 victory over Southampton – their biggest ever win in the Premiership. The match came just two months after Gerard Houllier assumed sole control of the team, and as he began imposing his own playing style.

The Frenchman was greatly helped not only by the presence of Fowler but of Michael Owen, who was also on the scoresheet that day. The two strikers still rank among the top 10 Premier League marksmen of all time. Fowler went on to score 163 goals in the top flight, while Owen had chalked up 150 when he retired at the end of the 2012–13 season.

RIGHT ROYAL ROUT

Liverpool's 6–1 thrashing of Hull City in September 2009 was watched by 44,392 people – including a senior member of the Saudi Royal Family. Crown Prince Faisal was at Anfield to enjoy the victory. Meanwhile the Kop celebrated not only a Fernando Torres hat-trick, but one of the best opening spells in the club's history. The team's tally of 22 goals in their opening seven League games that season was the best since 1895.

LEFT: Robbie ran riot: Three goals from Fowler sank the Saints in January 1999

BELOW: Hot shot: Michael Owen was Liverpool's leading goalscorer during the Gerard Houllier era

▶▶ GOAL NO. 1...AND NO. 100

Two of the club's record Premiership away victories were also milestones for two players. Former Everton defender Abel Xavier made his debut in the 6–0 win at Ipswich Town in February 2002, and opened the scoring after 16 minutes. It was his only Premiership goal for the Reds.

A year later Michael Owen was on target four times as the team put six past West Brom at the Hawthorns. His second of the afternoon saw him join the exclusive band of strikers to score 100 Premier League goals.

BIGGEST AWAY WINS – PREMIER LEAGUE

6–0 v Ipswich Town, 9 February 2002	
6–0 v West Bromwich Albion, 26 April 2003	
6–0 v Newcastle United, 27 April 2013	
6–1 v Crystal Palace, 20 August 1994	
5–0 v Swindon Town, 22 August 1993	
5–0 v West Bromwich Albion, 26 December 2004	

Biggest Defeats

◀◀ **CONTINUOUS LOSSES**

Liverpool's worst run of Premier League defeats came between February and April 2012 when they lost six out of seven League games. It was in the midst of this torrid period that the Reds also lifted the League Cup thanks to a penalty shoot-out victory over Cardiff at Wembley.

LOW POINTS

In 2011–12 Liverpool again sunk to an eighth place finish – their joint lowest since the launch of the Premiership. Kenny Dalglish's team recorded only six home wins all season, and picked up just 52 points from 38 matches, their lowest haul since the competition began.

RED CARDS AND RED FACES

Dismissals also played a part in two of Liverpool's other biggest Premier League defeats. In the 4–0 loss to Manchester United at Old Trafford in April 2003, Sami Hyypia was sent off after only three minutes. And in the 4–0 reverse away to Tottenham in September 2011 – Kenny Dalglish's worst result during his two spells as manager – the Reds ended the game with only nine men after Charlie Adam and Martin Skrtel had both received red cards.

ABOVE LEFT: Arsenal's Robin Van Persie piles on the misery during Liverpool's dismal 2012 Premier League run

LEFT: Chelsea's Didier Drogba scored twice in the 4–1 home loss in 2005

FAILURE AT FOREST

Liverpool's inaugural Premiership match against Nottingham Forest was the first to be televised live by Sky Sports. The game, which kicked off at 4pm on Sunday, 16 August 1992, also marked the start of Graeme Souness's first full season as manager. But his team made a bad start in front of the cameras, going down to a single Teddy Sheringham goal at the City Ground.

▶▶ **CHELSEA CURSE**

As well as inflicting two of Liverpool's biggest away defeats in the Premier League, Chelsea are also responsible for the worst result at Anfield. In October 2005 they beat the Reds 4–1 – their heaviest home League loss since Manchester United won by the same scoreline in 1969.

BIGGEST AWAY DEFEATS – PREMIERSHIP
1–5 v Coventry City, 19 December 1992
0–4 v Manchester United, 5 April 2003
0–4 v Chelsea, 16 December 2001
0–4 v Tottenham Hotspur, 18 September 2011
1–4 v Chelsea, 25 April 1998
1–4 v Blackburn Rovers, 3 April 1993

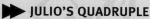

▶▶ JULIO'S QUADRUPLE

On 9 January 2007, Arsenal became the first team in 77 years to score six goals at Anfield. Their 6–3 League Cup Fifth Round victory was Liverpool's worst ever result in the competition, and the heaviest loss suffered by Rafael Benitez while he was manager.

Gunners' striker Julio Baptista scored four times – the first opposition striker to do so at Anfield since Wolves' Dennis Westcott 61 years previously. However, it took only two more years for another Arsenal forward to match Baptista's achievement. This time it was Andrei Arshavin, getting all his team's goals in a 4–4 Premier League draw.

SOUEY'S LAST SEASON

The Reds ended the 1993–94 season in eighth place – their worst position since winning promotion back to the top flight more than three decades previously. The poor finish was largely due to their away form which resulted in 11 defeats in 21 games. They also lost five times at Anfield and collected just 60 points from 42 matches. The season also brought disappointment in the knockout tournaments, and it was after a particularly embarrassing 1–0 loss to Bristol City in January 1994 that Graeme Souness left the manager's post to be replaced by Roy Evans.

ABOVE: Baptista on fire. The young Gunner fires one of his four League Cup tie goals at Anfield in January 2007

BELOW: Fans called him 'Hooperman' – but Mike was all too human in the 5–1 defeat by Coventry

PREMIER LEAGUE– MOST DEFEATS IN A SEASON

1993–94	16*
1992–93	15*
1998–99	14
2004–05	14
2010–11	14
2011–12	14

*42 matches played. The number of Premier League clubs was reduced from 22 to 20 at the start of the 1995–96 season, and the number of matches cut to 38.

▶▶ HIGHFIELD FIVE

The Premiership was just four months old when Liverpool were beaten 5–1 by Coventry City. More than two decades on, it remains the club's biggest defeat in the competition. Liverpool born strikers Mick Quinn and Brian Borrows did most of the damage at Highfield Road, hitting two goals apiece past goalkeeper Mike Hooper. Jamie Redknapp grabbed one back for the Reds, but then completed a miserable afternoon by being sent off.

BIGGEST HOME DEFEATS – PREMIER LEAGUE

1–4 v Chelsea, 2 October 2005	
1–3 v Leeds United, 14 November 1998	
1–3 v Aston Villa, 8 September 2001	
1–3 v Manchester United, 19 April 1997	
1–3 v Manchester United, 6 December 1997	
1–3 v Aston Villa, 24 August 2009	
1-3 v Aston Villa, 15 December, 2012	

Undefeated Records

▶▶ WINNING STREAK

The Reds' longest-ever winning run was in the 2005–06 season when they ended the campaign with 12 straight victories. The sequence culminated in a third place Premiership finish for Rafa Benitez and his team, and a dramatic penalty shoot-out triumph in the FA Cup. Discounting those spot-kicks in the final against West Ham, Liverpool scored 35 goals during the run, and conceded only 10.

Amazingly, the sequence continued into the next season, as the team's first two matches ended in victories against Maccabi Haifa in the Champions League, and Chelsea in the Community Shield.

THE WINNING HABIT

The record of 25 Premier League wins – set in 2005–06 – was equalled three season later. The Reds won 12 and drew seven of their 19 matches at Anfield , and also went on to pick up maximum points from 13 away games, matching a League record established more than a century earlier.

They finished the 2008–09 season as runners-up after scoring 77 Premier League goals and collecting 86 points – both club records.

ABOVE: Reina reigns supreme. Pepe kept the Reds' run intact at the 2006 FA Cup final

BELOW: Danny's the boy. Murphy's free kick sinks United in December 2000

▼ MURPHY'S SCORE

Rafael Benitez put Chelsea's long unbeaten home run to an end, but it was his predecessor who brought down the curtain on Manchester United's.

When Gerard Houllier took his side to Old Trafford on 17 December 2000, United had gone two years without a loss on home soil. Danny Murphy's expertly curled free kick ended all that – and secured Liverpool's first away victory over their great north-west rivals for a decade.

▶▶ HAPPY HUNTING GROUNDS

During the 2008–09 campaign the Reds collected more points on the road than in any other season in the top flight. They won 13 of their away matches, drew four and lost only two. Their most memorable away-days were at St. James' Park where they thrashed Newcastle 5–1, and at Old Trafford where they hammered Manchester United 4–1 – their best result at the ground since 1936.

Another notable victory came at Stamford Bridge on 26 October 2008, when Xabi Alonso's single goal brought an end to Chelsea's run of 86 home matches unbeaten – a record stretching back to 21 February 2004.

HOME COMFORTS

Liverpool reacted to their record home defeat to Chelsea by going on a record-breaking undefeated Premier League run at Anfield. The 4–1 reverse in October 2005 was followed by 30 successive Premier League games without loss. In December 2007 the team went on an even longer unbeaten run at home. The sequence lasted 31 games, including every Anfield Premier League match in the 2008–09 season. It ended in August 2009 with a 3–1 loss to Aston Villa.

PLUGGING THE LEAKS

As well as ending the 2005–06 season with a record-breaking winning run, the team began it by keeping four clean sheets in their opening four League games for the first time in the club's history. Between October and December they set a new record of 11 clean sheets, and went 762 minutes without conceding a League goal – a post-war club record.

GOAL-DEN START

The Reds began the 2009–10 season with 22 goals from their first seven League matches – their highest ever opening tally in the top flight. Fernando Torres contributed seven of them as the team beat the likes of Stoke and Burnley 4–0, and thrashed Hull City 6–1. They went on to break another record that season by scoring in their 18th successive Premier League match at Anfield.

MOST PREMIER LEAGUE AWAY POINTS

2008–09:	43 pts
2001–02:	39 pts
2005–06:	34 pts
2007–08:	34 pts
1996–97:	32 pts

ABOVE: Now, there's a sight you don't see every day...

RIGHT: 'Rafa the Gaffer'. Benitez masterminded two epic unbeaten runs during his spell as boss

RAFA'S DAZZLING DOZEN

Date	Opposition	Result	Competition
15/3/2006	Fulham (h)	5–1	Premier League
19/3/2006	Newcastle United (a)	3–1	Premier League
21/3/2006	Birmingham City (a)	7–0	FA Cup Sixth Round
25/3/2006	Everton (h)	3–1	Premier League
1/4/2006	West Bromwich Albion (a)	2–0	Premier League
9/4/2006	Bolton Wanderers (h)	1–0	Premier League
16/4/2006	Blackburn Rovers (a)	1–0	Premier League
22/4/2006	Chelsea (n)	2–1	FA Cup semi-final
26/4/2006	West Ham United (a)	2–1	Premier League
29/4/2006	Aston Villa (h)	3–1	Premier League
7/5/2006	Portsmouth (a)	3–1	Premier League
13/5/2006	West Ham United (n)	6–4*	FA Cup final

*3–3 at end of extra time, 3–1 on penalties

FA Cup & League Cup

Liverpool went 73 years without winning a major domestic knockout competition – but they've certainly made up for that barren spell since then.

Apart from lifting the FA Cup on seven occasions, the Reds have chalked up a remarkable League Cup record, winning the trophy an unprecedented eight times. League success will always be the club's priority but, for fans, collecting other silverware along the way is vitally important. As the saying goes: 'Liverpool FC is all about winning things and being a source of pride to its fans. It has no other purpose.'

BELOW: Counting the silverware. The Anfield trophy cabinet has been home to the most glittering 'knockout' prizes

FA Cup Winners

THE SAINT AND THE WINNER

The Wembley clash with Leeds was the first final to go to extra time for 28 years. Three minutes into the stoppage period, Roger Hunt broke the deadlock with a stooping header, only for his effort to be cancelled out by Billy Bremner's ferocious strike.

But with nine minutes left, Liverpool got the winner. It came from the head of Ian St. John, the striker who had arrived from Motherwell in a record £37,500 transfer deal four years earlier, and whose partnership with Hunt had proved prolific. 'The Saint' was a crowd favourite whose effort and commitment epitomised the never-say-die attitude of Shankly's sixties team. And the boss himself adored him. 'St. John is bubbling, skilful, courageous and non-stop – a footballer with a tiger in his tank,' wrote Shankly. 'He's a player who has the one thing so necessary for success: a heart the size of himself.'

KENNY'S FOREIGN LEGION

The 1986 Cup winning side was the first to contain no Englishmen. It was Welshman Ian Rush who took most of the plaudits, but two other 'foreigners' played huge parts in the victory.

Big Dane Jan Molby put in one of his greatest ever displays at Wembley, and capped a man-of-the-match performance by having a hand in the moves that led to all three Liverpool goals. And before that fight-back began, Zimbabwean goalkeeper Bruce Grobbelaar pulled off a phenomenal acrobatic save to prevent striker Graeme Sharp putting the Blues even further ahead. The ever-eccentric Grobbelaar ended the afternoon by doing part of the lap of honour on his hands.

SHANKS BOWS OUT

Nobody knew it at the time, but the 1974 final was to be Bill Shankly's last competitive game as manager. Just two months after collecting his sixth major trophy with Liverpool he stunned players, directors and fans by announcing his decision to quit.

▼ NEWCASTLE DOWN

Liverpool's second FA Cup success came courtesy of a 3–0 stroll against Newcastle United – one of the most one-sided finals in history. Kevin Keegan was the hero of the day, capping a man-of-the-match performance with two goals. In the Newcastle line-up for the 1974 Wembley clash were two players who would go on to have glittering careers at Anfield. Midfielder Terry McDermott joined the Reds just six months later, while left-back Alan Kennedy arrived in a £330,000 deal at the start of the 1978–79 season.

BELOW: Kevin's Cup. Keegan fires the first of his two goals in the 1974 Wembley victory over Newcastle

ABOVE: Gerry Byrne gets medical attention after the 1965 final. He played for 117 minutes with a broken collar bone

 TOUGH GUY, GERRY

Legendary Anfield hard man Tommy Smith rated Gerry Byrne as the toughest player he had ever met, and never was the full-back's bravery more evident than in the 1965 FA Cup final. Byrne broke his collar bone after just three minutes at Wembley but, with no substitutes allowed, chose to soldier on rather than allow the team to go down to 10 men.

RUSH AT THE DOUBLE

10 May 1986 was the day when Kenny Dalglish's first season as player-manager came to its triumphant climax. Having secured the League Championship one week earlier he led his side to an historic 'double' with victory over Everton in the first-ever all-Merseyside FA Cup final.

The Reds were outplayed for much of the first half, and it was no surprise when their rivals took a 27th minute lead through striker Gary Lineker. But they struck back with a vengeance after the interval, with Ian Rush equalising, Craig Johnston adding a second, and Rush putting the result beyond doubt with just six minutes left on the clock.

Defying excruciating pain, he put in a faultless defensive performance, and even got forward to supply the cross for Roger Hunt's opening goal. It wouldn't be the last act of heroism on Byrne's part. Less than a year later he dislocated an elbow in a European tie against Celtic but refused to leave the pitch until the 90 minutes were nearly up.

1965...AND ALL THAT

For Liverpudlians of a certain age, 1 May 1965 will always be among the most memorable dates in LFC's history. It was the day that Bill Shankly's team ended an FA Cup hoodoo that had lasted more than seven decades, and led to years of mockery from the 'blue' half of Merseyside. But, following a 2–1 triumph over Leeds, the FA Cup was finally bound for the Anfield trophy cabinet. Never would Reds' fans be subject to such taunts again.

THE YEAR OF THE SCOTS

St. John was one of four Scotsmen in the line-up for the first Wembley triumph. The others were keeper Tommy Lawrence, defender Ron Yeats and midfielder Willie Stevenson. Their shirt numbers were 1, 9, 6 and 5.

SUBS MAKE HISTORY

Everton's Stuart McCall made FA Cup history in 1989 by becoming the first substitute to score twice in the final of the tournament. But his achievement remained unique for just 120 seconds – which was how long it took Rush to grab his second of the afternoon.

◀◀ MERSEYSIDE UNITED

The 1989 FA Cup final brought the two Merseyside footballing giants together on an emotional day just five weeks after the Hillsborough disaster. It was an afternoon when both the clubs and their supporters displayed a poignant togetherness, with a rousing joint rendition of 'You'll Never Walk Alone' before the kick-off.

The match itself was one of the most exciting finals for years. John Aldridge made up for his previous year's penalty miss against Wimbledon by opening the scoring after just four minutes, only to see his potential winner cancelled out in the dying stages.

It was left to Ian Rush, sent on as Aldridge's replacement, to secure the trophy, scoring twice in extra time, and overtaking Dixie Dean's record of 19 goals in Merseyside derbies. Everton had equalised after his first, but the Welshman put the game beyond them just two minutes later.

LEFT: Ian Rush beats Everton's Neville Southall to help seal Wembley victory in 1989

BELOW: Owen's goal. The striker slots home the 2001 FA Cup final winner against Arsenal in Cardiff

▼ MICHAEL – PRINCE OF WALES

The Reds' 2–1 victory in the 2001 final was a case of third time lucky: twice they had faced Arsenal at the same stage of the competition, and twice they had lost. But this time they had Michael Owen in the side. The Chester-born striker was in the form of his life, enjoying the first of his three most prolific seasons at Anfield. And, at Cardiff, he turned in one of the virtuoso displays that brought him the coveted Ballon D'Or later that year.

Even the most ardent Liverpudlian had to agree that their team were second best for most of the afternoon, and that Arsenal were worth their one-goal lead. But Owen's pace and deadly eye for goal changed everything. With seven minutes left he equalised with an instinctive shot on the turn. Then, just two minutes from time, he outran the Gunners' defence to rifle an angled winner past England keeper David Seaman.

This remains the only FA Cup final that Liverpool have won while wearing an 'away' strip. After Arsenal won the right to wear red and white, Owen and co turned out in gold and navy.

▶▶ REINA IS THE SHOOT-OUT HERO

As well as playing in the first FA Cup final at the Millennium Stadium, Liverpool also took part in the last. Once again they returned from Cardiff victorious.

The 2006 clash with West Ham became known, in some quarters, as 'The Gerrard Final', because of the way the Reds' captain inspired a brilliant fight-back, equalising twice to force a 3–3 draw at the end of full-time. But it was the heroics from Pepe Reina that did most to secure victory in the subsequent penalty shoot-out.

The Spaniard saved three of the Londoners' four spot-kicks, denying Bobby Zamora, Paul Konchesky and Anton Ferdinand. Liverpool, meanwhile, converted three, courtesy of Didi Hamann, John Arne Riise and Gerrard.

RIGHT: A beaming Pepe Reina after his shoot-out heroics in the 2006 final

CARDIFF CALLING

The redevelopment of Wembley meant the 2001 FA Cup final was staged outside England for the first time in the competition's history. The venue for the Liverpool v Arsenal clash was Cardiff's Millennium Stadium, where the Reds had lifted the League Cup just three months earlier. With Gerard Houllier and Arsene Wenger in the dug-outs, it was also the first FA Cup final in which the managers of both teams were from outside the British isles.

MEDALS MIX UP

The Reds may have won the 1992 final, but they came down the Wembley steps clutching losers' medals. The FA gave the two teams the wrong sets during the post-match presentation, and the Liverpool and Sunderland players later had to exchange them on the pitch.

▶▶ SUCCESS FOR SOUNESS

Boss Graeme Souness was admitted to hospital for heart surgery after Liverpool's 1–1 FA Cup semi-final draw with Portsmouth in 1992. As the Reds won the replay – the first-ever to be decided on penalties – he had to watch it on television.

Doctors warned the manager to stay away from the clash with Sunderland, fearing the stress would hinder his recovery. But Souness, who never reached the FA Cup final as a player, defied their advice. He left it to his assistant Ronnie Moran to lead the team out, but gave a ferocious half-time team talk after seeing his players outplayed in the opening 45 minutes. The tactic worked. As club doctor Bill Reid kept a restraining hand on the manager in the dug-out, Liverpool scored twice through Michael Thomas and Ian Rush. It was Rush's fifth goal in FA Cup finals – an achievement no other player has matched.

ABOVE: Boss Souness is flanked by medical staff as he walks to the Wembley dug-out in 1992

FA Cup Miscellaneous

WATERSHED AT WATFORD

A 1–0 defeat at Second Division Watford in 1970 prompted Bill Shankly to dismantle his sixties side and begin building a team that would dominate the next decade.

Among the immediate casualties of that shock FA Cup quarter-final loss were goalkeeper Tommy Lawrence, centre-back Ron Yeats and striker Ian St. John. 'Watford was the crucial game,' the manager later wrote. 'I could see that a few of the players had started to go a bit. It was obvious that while some still had an appetite for success, others hadn't, and might do better elsewhere.'

WORCESTER WOE

Liverpool have faced non-League sides five times in the FA Cup since World War II. They overcame Altrincham in 1981, Yeovil Town in 2004, Havant & Waterlooville in 2008 and Mansfield Town in 2013.

On 15 January 1959, another team of part-timers dealt the Reds their worst ever result in the competition. Worcester City, then of the Southern League, beat them 2–1 in front of a record 15,000 crowd at their St. George's Lane ground. Even though Liverpool were then in the Second Division it remains one of the biggest upsets in FA Cup history.

BELOW: Whose goal was it? Arsenal celebrate their equaliser in the 1971 final, as Reds skipper Tommy Smith appeals for offside

GOING THE EXTRA ROUND

Liverpool were once forced to play an extra round in the FA Cup as punishment for failing to submit their entry for the competition before the deadline. The so-called 'Supplementary Round' took place at West Ham's Canning Town ground on 5 January 1901. A single goal from Sam Raybould was enough to sink the Hammers, but Liverpool then lost their First Round tie against Notts County.

▼ GUNNED DOWN

Charlie George's long-range winner for Arsenal over Liverpool in the 1971 FA Cup final may be one of the most famous Wembley goals of all time, but it was the Gunners' earlier equaliser that proved to be historic. Although originally credited to George Graham, TV replays showed the final touch came from Eddie Kelly – making him the first substitute to score in a final.

LONGEST MATCH

The epic 1980 FA Cup semi-final against Arsenal ranks as the longest match in the history of the club, as well as the tournament itself. Following a dour 0–0 draw at Hillsborough, it took three replays – the first two going to extra time – for the tie to be settled. When the whistle blew at the end of the third re-match at Highfield Road, the two teams had played for 420 minutes – but it was Arsenal who went through thanks to a single goal in the last 90. Prior to the game, no FA Cup semi-final had gone beyond two replays. And none will do so in future. In 1992, the FA introduced the penalty shoot-out to settle deadlocked ties.

MILESTONE GOALS

Scottish international Tom Wylie grabbed Liverpool's first FA Cup goal, opening the scoring in a 4–0 victory over Nantwich on 15 October 1892. By the end of the 2012–13 season they had scored 692 goals in the competition, with the last coming from Joe Allen in a Fourth Round defeat at Oldham. Other milestone goals include:

100th: Arthur Goddard (v Gainsborough Trinity, 14 January 1911)
200th: Syd Roberts (v Yeovil & Petters Utd, 12 January 1935)
300th: Roger Hunt (v Wrexham, 9 January 1963)
400th: Steve Heighway (v Carlisle United, 29 January 1977)
500th: Craig Johnston (v Manchester City, 13 March 1988)
600th: Jamie Redknapp (v Coventry City, 3 January 1998)

THE 4–4 TWO

The Reds reached their first FA Cup semi-final in 1899, only to be beaten by Sheffield United in a second replay. The first one ended 4–4 – a Cup scoreline that wasn't repeated until 1991 when Kenny Dalglish's team took on Everton in a Fifth Round replay at Goodison Park. The match is remembered as one of the most exciting Merseyside derbies ever – and for being Dalglish's final game during his first spell as manager.

BEWARE OF BOLTON!

Bolton Wanderers are responsible for two of Liverpool's three heaviest FA Cup defeats. They won a 1946 Fourth Round tie 5–0 at Burnden Park, 17 years after delivering a 5–2 thrashing at the same venue. Liverpool's biggest home defeat came in 1898 when Derby County hammered the Reds 5–1 in a Third round replay.

▼ ONE OVER THE EIGHT

The 9–0 win over Welsh side Newtown in Liverpool's first-ever season remains a club record in the FA Cup. The Reds came nearest to matching it in January 1990 when they thumped Swansea 8–0 in a Third Round replay at Anfield.

In 2006, Rafa Benitez's side despatched Birmingham at St. Andrews, setting a new record for an away victory in the competition. Sami Hyypia opened the scoring in the first minute, then a brace from Peter Crouch, and further strikes from Fernando Morientes, John Arne Riise and Djibril Cisse – plus an own goal – made it 7–0.

BELOW: Sami Hyypia (second left) sets the Reds on their way to a crushing 7–1 FA Cup away win at Birmingham

BIGGEST WINS – FA CUP

Opposition	Result	Round	Date
Newtown (h)	9–0	Qualifier	29/10/1892
Swansea City (h)	8–0	3 (replay)	9/1/1990
York City (h)	7–0	5 (replay)	20/2/1985
Rochdale (h)	7–0	3 (replay)	6/1/1996
Birmingham City (a)	7–0	6	21/3/2006

League Cup Winners

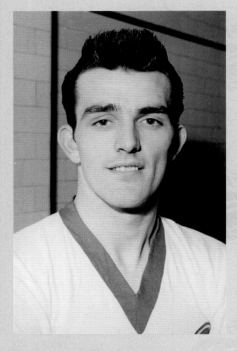

◀◀ A FINAL GESTURE

Reds fans remember the 1983 final against Manchester United for Ronnie Whelan's sublime curled shot that secured a 2–1 extra-time victory. Historians remember it as the only Wembley final in which a manager, rather than a captain, went up to collect the trophy.

With Liverpool already out of that season's FA Cup, and Bob Paisley just months from retirement, this was destined to be his last appearance at the old stadium. Skipper Graeme Souness marked the occasion by insisting his boss lifted the trophy.

IN THE BEGINNING

The League Cup was founded in the 1960–61 season so clubs could exploit the opportunities offered by recently installed floodlights. Liverpool's first match was against Luton Town on 19 October 1960. It ended 1–1 in front of a 10,502 crowd at Anfield, with Tommy Leishman getting the Reds' first-ever goal. By the end of the 2012–13 season they had scored 432 times in the competition.

LEFT: Scotsman Tommy Leishman scored Liverpool's first-ever League Cup goal, in a 1–1 draw against Luton Town at Anfield in October 1960. The Reds won the replay 5–2

BELOW: Phil Thompson in jubilant mood after the victory over West Ham at Villa Park in 1981. He was the first Reds skipper to lift the League Cup

STAND UP FOR THE BOSS

Tottenham went into the 1982 tournament having never lost a final at Wembley. At 1–0 up, with just three minutes left, and with Ray Clemence in their goal, they looked certain to preserve their record. But then Ronnie Whelan struck a brilliant equaliser, and manager Bob Paisley played a psychological masterstroke.

'He wouldn't let us sit down before extra time started,' recalled full-back Phil Neal. 'He was shouting: "Get up on your feet, don't them let them see you are tired." It stemmed from Shankly, who would never let an opponent see that you were weak. After that, we felt we had it in the bag.' And they were right. As the game wore on, the Spurs team tired and Liverpool forged ahead thanks to a second from Whelan and a clincher from Ian Rush.

▶▶ NAME THAT CUP

For the 1981–82 season, the Football League decided that the tournament should be referred to by the name of its then sponsor, the Milk Marketing Board. Various other sponsors have followed and the Cup has gone under several different names in the eight years that Liverpool have won it. They are:

1981: League Cup	1995: Coca Cola Cup
1982: Milk Cup	2001: Worthington Cup
1983: Milk Cup	2003: Worthington Cup
1984: Milk Cup	2012: Carling Cup

MILESTONE GOALS – LEAGUE CUP

100th: Kenny Dalglish (v Birmingham City, 2 December 1980)
200th: John Wark (v Fulham, 23 September 1986)
300th: Robbie Fowler (v Crystal Palace, 8 March 1995)
400th: Steven Gerrard (v Arsenal, 9 January 2007)

THE FIRST FINALS

The Reds' first League Cup final in 1978 ended in bitter disappointment and controversy, as they lost a replay to Nottingham Forest at Old Trafford. Bob Paisley's team had dominated the Wembley tie but were denied by the brilliance of 18-year-old Chris Woods, then the youngest goalkeeper to have taken part in a major final. Liverpool also had the better of the re-match but lost because of a penalty awarded for a foul that – TV replays proved – had taken place outside the box.

It was another three years before they got the chance to ease their disappointment, and once again the final had to go to a replay. After West Ham grabbed a last minute equaliser at Wembley, the two teams headed to Villa Park where goals from Kenny Dalglish and Alan Hansen secured a 2–1 victory.

THE LOST YEARS

After going out to Southampton at the Third Round stage in 1960, Liverpool didn't bother entering again for another seven years – by which time the League Cup winners were guaranteed a place in Europe. It may have taken 14 more years to finally get their hands on the trophy, but the Reds have since become the most successful team in the history of the tournament, playing in more finals and lifting the Cup on more occasions than anyone else.

ABOVE: Paisley's pride. The manager went up the Wembley steps to receive the trophy in 1983

THE FIRST MERSEYSIDE FINAL

Few Merseyside derbies have raised excitement levels as much as the 1984 League Cup final – the first-ever meeting between Liverpool and Everton at Wembley. Even fewer have combined intense rivalry with such a spirit of friendliness.

The match, played against a backdrop of severe economic recession in Liverpool and its surrounding areas, proved to be a PR triumph for the city, with tens of thousands of opposing fans travelling to London together, and standing side by side on the terraces. At the end of the 0–0 draw, the two teams completed a joint lap of honour to a rousing chant of 'Merseyside, Merseyside'. The Metropolitan police, who had been geared for possible trouble, described it as the 'the friendliest final' in years.

Three days later the teams met again at Maine Road where a dipping shot from Graeme Souness settled matters. It was Liverpool's first trophy of the season – but two more were soon to follow.

BELOW: Merseyside United. The Reds and the Blues after their deadlocked 1984 final at Wembley

RAFA V. JOSE

The 2005 final also brought together Rafa Benitez and Jose Mourinho, the two managers who had led their previous clubs – Valencia and Porto – to UEFA and European Cup success, respectively, a year earlier. Mourinho may have won on the day but he also collected the dubious distinction of becoming the only boss to be dismissed during an English domestic final. When the Portuguese celebrated his side's equaliser by putting a finger to his lips in front of the Liverpool crowd, the referee decided it was a 'provocative gesture' – and banished him to the dressing room.

◀◀ ONE DOWN, TWO TO GO

The 2001 League Cup final was the first to be played at the Millennium Stadium, and the first to be decided on penalties. Liverpool had looked on course for a 1–0 victory over Birmingham thanks to Robbie Fowler's first-half 25-yard volley, but then Darren Purse equalised in the 90th minute.

After extra-time deadlock, the match went to a shoot-out. Liverpool scored four times from the spot, while Sander Westerveld pulled off two magnificent saves to help land the club's first silverware in six years. It was only the beginning, though. By the end of the season Gerard Houllier's team had added the FA and UEFA Cups to the Anfield trophy cabinet.

▼ COMPLETING THE COLLECTION

The League Cup was the one major domestic honour to elude Kenny Dalglish during his first spell as LFC manager. But he made up for that omission during his first full season back in charge.

Still, it was a close run thing. Dalglish's team only lifted the 2012 trophy following a penalty shoot-out against Cardiff City who had held them to a 2–2 draw at the end of extra time at Wembley. Despite Steven Gerrard and Charlie Adam missing the first two of Liverpool's spot-kicks, they still managed to win – thanks to Cardiff missing three of theirs.

ABOVE: Steven Gerrard celebrates his deflected opener in the 2003 final against Man United

UNITED THEY FALL

Nearly two years after sinking Arsenal in the 2001 FA Cup final, Michael Owen returned to the Millennium Stadium to seal victory against Manchester United in the League Cup. His 86th minute strike followed Steven Gerrard's deflected first-half effort to give the Reds a 2–0 win. But it was keeper Jerzy Dudek who earned most of the plaudits with a series of brilliant saves to deny United's forwards.

THE CUP RUNNETH...AND RUNNETH

Liverpool's 1–0 Third Round defeat by Tottenham on 31 October 1984 brought the League Cup's longest-ever unbeaten run to an end. It was the first time Liverpool had lost in the competition since 12 February 1980, when they went out to Nottingham Forest at the semi-final stage.

RIISE'S ROAR

John Arne Riise's opening goal in the 2005 Millennium Stadium clash with Chelsea was the fastest in a League Cup final. It also created the loudest noise ever recorded at any sporting event in the world. The roar that greeted his volley just 45 seconds after kick-off was officially measured at 130.7 decibels – the equivalent of the noise when standing next to a pneumatic drill.

Sadly, it wasn't enough to secure victory. Chelsea equalised through a Steven Gerrard own goal, then added two more in extra time. The Reds did pull one back thanks to Spanish forward Antonio Nunez – who became the only Liverpool player to score his only goal for the club in a cup final.

GOALS GOALS GOALS

Four goals from Steve McMahon helped Liverpool to a 10–0 win over Fulham in September 1986 – the joint highest victory in the history of the competition. They went on to win the second leg 3–2, equalling the record 11-goal aggregate victory they set in 1981 with 5–0 and 6–0 wins over Exeter City at Anfield and St. James' Park.

In November 2000, they also equalled the record for the highest away win in the tournament, beating Stoke City 8–0 at the Britannia Stadium. Robbie Fowler did most of the damage that night, netting a hat-trick.

▼ THANK EVANS FOR MACCA

Roy Evans won the League Cup at his first attempt, but it was to be the only trophy he lifted as manager. His 1995 success was largely thanks to the brilliance of Steve McManaman, whose wonderful solo goals secured the Reds' 2–1 win over Bolton Wanderers.

BELOW: McManaman of the Match ... and Steve scored both goals in the 1995 League Cup final victory over Bolton

BIGGEST WINS – LEAGUE CUP

Opposition	Result	Round	Date
Fulham (h)	10–0	2 (1st Leg)	23/9/1986
Stoke City (a)	8–0	4	29/11/2000
Exeter City (a)	6–0	2 (2nd Leg)	28/10/1981
Swindon Town (h)	5–0	3	23/9/1980
Exeter City (h)	5–0	2 (1st Leg)	7/10/1981
Fulham (h)	5–0	2 (2nd Leg)	5/10/1993
Crystal Palace (h)	5–0	Semi-final (2nd Leg)	24/1/2001

European Competition

THREE TIME LOSERS

The Cup Winners' Cup is the one European trophy Liverpool have never won – and never will. They almost did manage it in 1966 when they went all the way to the final against Borussia Dortmund at Hampden Park. Roger Hunt cancelled out Dortmund's opener with the Reds' first-ever goal in a European final, but an extra-time own goal from Ron Yeats swung the result the Germans' way.

Liverpool competed for the trophy four more times, getting as far as the semi-finals in 1997. In 1999 the tournament was staged for the last time. Since then, the winners of each country's main domestic knockout competition have been entered into the UEFA Cup (later the Europa League).

The Reds' two other final losses were both in the European Cup. In 1985, they lost 1–0 to Juventus in a match overshadowed by the tragedy that unfolded inside Belgium's Heysel Stadium. And in 2007 they lost 2–1 to AC Milan in Athens – a result that denied Rafa Benitez his second Champions League success in three years.

▼ SUPER REDS

To add to their eight major European trophies, Liverpool have also won three Super Cups. The trophy – contested between the holders of the European and UEFA Cups – was first won in 1977, thanks to a thumping 7–1 two-legged victory over Hamburg. Further triumphs followed in 2001, when Gerard Houllier's side beat Bayern Munich 3–2 at the Stade Louis II in Monaco, to take their fifth trophy in six months. And in 2005 when Rafa Benitez masterminded a 3–1 win over CSKA Moscow at the same venue.

THE FIRST STEPS

It's now almost 50 years since Bill Shankly took a Liverpool team into European competition for the first time. That season's adventure began in the amateur footballing backwater of Iceland and ended in the cauldron of one of world's greatest sporting arenas: the San Siro, home of the then European champions, Inter Milan.

The Reds exited the European Cup in controversial circumstances that night in May 1965, falling victim to intense crowd hostility and a series of questionable refereeing decisions. But the sour taste of semi-final defeat was soon forgotten. For players and fans, eyes had been opened, horizons widened and ambitions lifted. Success was no longer restricted to beating rivals in England. It was about overcoming the elite of the continent.

BELOW: Three-time winners. The Reds lift their third UEFA Super Cup in Monaco in 2005

WINNERS
UEFA SUPER CUP 2005

tory over CSKA Moscow in the UEFA Super Cup at the Stade Louis II, in Monaco, on Thursday 25 August 2005. Liverpool won 3 - 1 after extra-time.

PAISLEY, THE MASTER

Shankly was the pioneer whose teams qualified for Europe for 11 consecutive seasons. He studied the continental style intensely, and put new tactics of containment and counter-attack into practice. But despite some epic runs and unforgettable games, he only managed to win one European trophy: the 1973 UEFA Cup. It was his successor Bob Paisley who proved to be the master tactician, capable of outflanking the continent's leading coaches season after season. Just two years in to the job he landed the club's second UEFA Cup. Twelve months on, he won the first of his three European Cups – an achievement that remains unique.

BRITAIN'S BEST

The statistics show how Liverpool have risen to that challenge. Since first qualifying in 1964, they have competed in Europe for 39 seasons, 21 of them consecutively. They have fought their way to 11 finals, winning eight. They have lifted the UEFA Cup on three occasions, a joint record. Most impressive of all, they have won the European Cup five times – a towering achievement no other British club comes close to matching. In fact, of all clubs in Europe only Real Madrid and AC Milan have been more successful in the elite competition and Bayern Munich are equal.

ABOVE: The first European success. Bill Shankly with the UEFA Cup in 1973

FIXTURES NEAR AND FAR

The Reds have competed in 38 countries, including England, in their five decades of European action. They have faced German opposition 36 times and Spanish teams on 32 occasions. Nearer to home, they've been drawn against clubs from Northern Ireland and Wales only once each. They met Crusaders in the First Round of the 1976–77 European Cup, and Total Network Solutions in the qualifying rounds of the 2005–06 Champions League.

RED ALERT

On 25 November 1964, Bill Shankly sent his team out in all-red for the first time. During preparations for a European Cup tie against Anderlecht, the manager was convinced the new colour scheme would make his players appear bigger and more intimidating on the field. The 3–0 victory over the Belgian champions confirmed his view. At the end of the season, in which Liverpool also clinched their first FA Cup dressed in all-red, the old white shorts and socks were consigned to the dustbin.

BELOW: Staying power. Three of Liverpool's greatest servants, Tommy Smith, Ian Callaghan and Phil Neal, with the European Cup after the 3–1 victory over Borussia Moenchengladbach at Rome in 1977

EUROPE – HOW THE MANAGERS MEASURE UP

Bob Paisley:	3 European Cups, 1 UEFA Cup, 1 Super Cup
Rafael Benitez:	1 European Cup, 1 Super Cup
Joe Fagan:	1 European Cup
Gerard Houllier:	1 UEFA Cup, 1 Super Cup
Bill Shankly:	1 UEFA Cup

Biggest Wins

BAD LUCK OF THE IRISH

The 1969 Fairs Cup tie against Irish League side Dundalk was only Ray Clemence's second outing for Liverpool. But any attempts to assess his skills were useless, as the Reds' keeper hardly saw the ball all night. Instead, the action was confined to the other end, where his opposite number, Maurice Swan, picked the ball out of the net 10 times.

This was only the second time that Liverpool reached double figures in one match. And, when the sides met at Oriel Park two weeks later, they made history again. By scoring four times without reply they recorded a 14–0 victory over the two legs – their highest aggregate win in any competition before or since.

◄◄ FIRST ELEVEN

It didn't take Bob Paisley long to make history in European competition: in his first game as boss, his team broke Liverpool's all-time scoring record. A crowd of 24,743 were there to see the Reds take on Norwegian part-timers Stromsgodset on 17 September 1974. But if most believed victory was a foregone conclusion, none could have foreseen the rout that unfolded on the Anfield pitch.

The Cup Winners' Cup First Round tie was just three minutes old when left-back Alec Lindsay scored from the penalty spot. By half-time Liverpool were 5–0 up thanks to a brace from Phil Boersma and a goal apiece from Phil Thompson and Steve Heighway. The interval may have brought some relief to the visitors, but the second period was to prove even worse. The Reds hit six more, as Thompson weighed in with a second, and Peter Cormack, Emlyn Hughes, Tommy Smith, Ian Callaghan and Ray Kennedy all joined in the fun.

LEFT: Phil Thompson was on target twice in the Reds' biggest-ever win

RIGHT: Yossi Benayoun celebrates his hat-trick in the record Champions League win over Besiktas

▼ BESIKTAS BITE THE DUST

Rafa Benitez marked his 50th Champions League game with Liverpool by delivering the biggest ever victory in the competition outside the preliminary stages. His team had looked like candidates for an early exit from the tournament after losing 2–1 away to Besiktas. But when the Turkish side came to Anfield, the Reds responded with an awesome display and an 8–0 victory. An inspirational Steven Gerrard, who had been on target in the first leg, got one of the goals, while Peter Crouch and Ryan Babel grabbed two each. But the star performance came from Yossi Benayoun who hit the first of his three hat-tricks for the club.

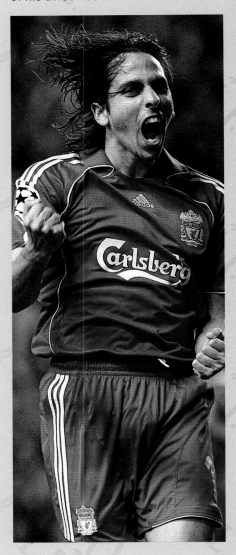

RUSHIE OFF THE MARK

Just a year after the Reds' 10–1 destruction of Oulu Palloseura, the two sides met again, and at the same stage of the European Cup. This time the scoreline was a relatively modest 7–0, with Mark Lawrenson scoring on his debut, and young substitute Ian Rush getting the first of his record 346 goals for the club.

▼ HAT-TRICK HEROES

Finnish Champions Oulu Palloseura had held the Reds to a 1–1 draw in the home leg of the 1980–81 European Cup First Round. But their dreams of an upset were quickly dispelled at Anfield as Liverpool embarked on a ruthlessly professional demolition. David Fairclough, Sammy Lee and Ray Kennedy all got their names on the scoresheet in the 10–1 victory, but the stars of the night were Graeme Souness and Terry McDermott with three goals apiece. This was only the third time in the club's history that two LFC players had bagged hat-tricks in the same match – and it came 53 years to the day (1 October) after the previous occurrence.

RIGHT: Souness strikes. The captain was one of two players to get hat-tricks against Finnish champions Oulu Palloseura

BIGGEST HOME WINS – EUROPE

Opposition	Result	Competition	Date
Stromsgodset	11–0	Cup Winners' Cup (R1, 1st Leg)	17/9/1974
Dundalk	10–0	Fairs Cup (R1, 1st Leg)	16/9/1969
Oulu Palloseura	10–1	European Cup (R1, 2nd Leg)	1/10/1980
TSV Munich	8–0	Fairs Cup (R2, 1st Leg)	7/11/1967
Besiktas	8–0	Champions League (1st Group Phase)	6/11/2007

BIGGEST AWAY WINS – EUROPE

Opposition	Result	Competition	Date
KR Reykjavik	5–0	European Cup (Prelim 1st Leg)	17/8/1964
Crusaders	5–0	European Cup (R1, 2nd Leg)	28/9/1976
FC Haka	5–0	Champions League (Qualifier 1st Leg)	8/8/2001
Dundalk	4–0	Fairs Cup (R1 2nd Leg)	30/9/1969
Marseilles	4–0	Champions League (1st Group Phase)	11/12/2007

ROGER'S RECORD

Liverpool's 8–0 hammering of TSV Munich in 1967 remains their highest victory over German opponents. Roger Hunt scored twice in the Fairs Cup tie at Anfield, to surpass Gordon Hodgson's 32-year-old record of 241 goals for the club.

Munich's goalkeeper was the Yugoslav international, and part-time pop singer, Petar Radenkovic, often referred to as one of the world's best stoppers. He was renowned for denying strikers with acrobatic saves, and took pride in his personal motto: 'never more than one a match'. But after this particular game he wisely left the quotes to club president Albert Wetzel, who reflected on Liverpool's attacking prowess: 'I have never seen a team shoot with such power from any position.'

Biggest Defeats

ANNIHILATION BY AJAX

The 'total football' made famous by Holland coach Rinus Michels reached its breathtaking height at the 1974 World Cup finals. But it had its origins on a foggy night in Amsterdam eight years earlier when his club side Ajax took on Liverpool in a European Cup Second Round tie.

A 19-year-old prodigy named Johann Cruyff was in the line-up that evening, as the Dutch champions put Michels' pioneering tactics into practice, freely exchanging positions throughout the 90 minutes. And the results were devastating. At half-time, they were 4–0 up. By the final whistle they had added a fifth, with the visitors managing to pull just one goal back at the death.

NO WAY BACK

The 5–1 loss at Ajax was Liverpool's heaviest in European competition, but boss Bill Shankly was keen to explain it away as a fluke, the result of the mist which grew so thick that his players couldn't even see each other as the game wore on. He predicted a 7–0 Reds' victory in the second leg, and spoke with such confidence and conviction that his players and supporters all believed him. On the night of the return match, Anfield was packed to the gills with nearly 54,000 fans.

But the promised fight-back never materialised. Cruyff scored twice to silence the Kop, and although Roger Hunt hit two goals in return, Liverpool went down 7–3 on aggregate – their worst ever defeat over two legs. Ajax returned to find thousands of fans lining the streets of Amsterdam to welcome them home.

FALLING FOUL OF THE RULES

UEFA ended the tradition of deciding deadlocked games by the toss of a coin at the end of the 1967–68 season – just after Liverpool went out of the Fairs Cup to Atletico Bilbao via that method. In its place came the rule that away goals should count double in the event of a draw.

The following season, the Reds beat Vittoria Setubal 3–2 at Anfield after losing the first leg in Portugal 1–0. Confusingly, nobody had properly explained the new rule to the players or supporters, both of whom were expecting the game to go into extra time once the whistle blew on 90 minutes. It took a lengthy explanation from the referee, and a public address announcement, to convince the 41,000 fans that their Fairs Cup adventure was over for a second year running.

FIRST FOR FERENCVAROS

Liverpool played in Europe for more than three years before suffering their first home defeat. That came at the hands of Hungarian side Ferencvaros who followed up their Fairs Cup Third Round 1–0 victory in Budapest with a win by the same scoreline at Anfield in January 1968.

▼ SPARTAK SORROW

As well as being responsible for one of Liverpool's worst home losses in Europe, Spartak Moscow also inflicted an embarrassingly heavy aggregate defeat. In October 1992, Liverpool were just six minutes from earning a creditable 2–2 draw in the away leg of the Cup Winners' Cup second round. But then came keeper Bruce Grobbelaar's dismissal after all the available substitutes had been used. Full-back David Burrows, who was forced to don the keeper's jersey, was beaten by a penalty and a fourth Spartak goal a minute from time. Manager Graeme Souness was incensed by the sending off, and protested so vehemently with the referee that he was suspended from the touchline and directors' box for the Anfield re-match. It was just as well he didn't watch, as his team were outclassed. Spartak came away with a 2–0 win on the night and a 6–2 victory over the two legs.

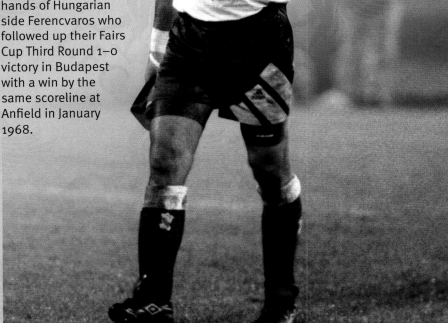

RIGHT: Brucie gets the blues after his red card in Moscow

Chelsea are the only other team to put seven past Liverpool over two legs in Europe. In 2009 they won the Champions League quarter-final first leg 3–1 at Anfield, then repelled a spirited fight-back at Stamford Bridge to finish the return match 4–4. The Londoners are one of only five sides to win a European match at Anfield by a margin of two goals.

RIGHT: Steven Gerrard tussles with Michael Ballack in the 3–1 loss to Chelsea, the Reds' only loss at Anfield in 2008–09

BIGGEST HOME DEFEATS – EUROPE

Opposition	Result	Competition	Date
Spartak Moscow	0-2	Cup Winners' Cup (R2, 2nd Leg)	4/11/1992
Barcelona	1–3	Champions League (2nd Group Phase)	20/11/2001
Celtic	0–2	UEFA Cup (R5, 2nd Leg)	20/3/2003
Benfica	0–2	Champions League (R1, 2nd Leg)	8/3/2006
Chelsea	1–3	Champions League (QF, 1st Leg)	8/4/2009

BIGGEST AWAY DEFEATS – EUROPE

Opposition	Result	Competition	Date
Ajax	1–5	European Cup (R2, 1st Leg)	7/12/1966
Inter Milan	0–3	European Cup (SF, 2nd Leg)	12/5/1965
Dinamo Tblisi	0–3	European Cup (R1, 2nd Leg)	3/10/1979
Paris Saint-Germain	0–3	Cup Winners' Cup (SF, 1st Leg)	10/4/1997
Strasbourg	0-3	UEFA Cup (R2, 1st Leg)	21/10/1997

UEFA Cup Winners

'GOLDEN GOAL' – A BRIEF HISTORY

FIFA introduced the 'golden goal' rule in 1993 in the hope that it would lead to more attacking football during extra time, and therefore fewer penalty shoot-outs. However, it wasn't compulsory, and it was up to individual competitions whether to apply it.

The first major international tournament to be decided under the system was Euro 96, when Germany beat the Czech Republic in the final with a goal five minutes into extra time. France's victories over Paraguay at the 1998 World Cup, and Italy at Euro 2000, were both thanks to 'golden goals'.

Only two European club tournaments were ever settled under the controversial rule. Liverpool's UEFA Cup final against Alaves, and Galatasaray's Super Cup win over Real Madrid the previous year. In 2004 the 'golden goal' was removed from the Laws of the Game.

THE SECOND DOUBLE...

The Reds completed a second League and UEFA Cup double just three years later, thanks to another two legged victory – this time over FC Bruges. The Belgians stunned the Kop by going 2–0 up within 15 minutes of the opening match. But that merely provided the cue for a magical Anfield night when the crowd inspired the team to do the seemingly impossible. By the 61st minute Liverpool were level thanks to goals from Ray Kennedy and Jimmy Case; by the 64th they were ahead, courtesy of a Kevin Keegan penalty.

Two weeks later, and with the League title wrapped up, 'Player of the Year' Keegan sealed the victory in Belgium by equalising the home side's opening goal. The trophy was on its way to Anfield again – and 'Manager of the Year' Bob Paisley was on his way to becoming Europe's most successful boss.

BELOW: That completes the treble. The Reds add the UEFA Cup to their League Cup and FA Cup successes earlier in 2001

▼ ...AND THE FIRST TREBLE

The 2001 UEFA Cup final against Alaves was the highest-scoring in the tournament's history – and the only one to be decided by a 'golden goal'. For the 30,000 Liverpudlians in the Wesfalenstadion – and the millions watching on television – it was one of the most memorable finals ever.

After leading through early goals from Markus Babbel and Steven Gerrard, Liverpool seemed to be coasting. Even after Alaves pulled one back, a Gary McAllister penalty looked to have put the game beyond their reach. But then the Spaniards roared back with two goals after the break. Robbie Fowler re-established the Reds' lead, only to see it cancelled out by a last minute strike.

With the score at 4–4 the game went into extra time, destined to be decided by the next goal. In the event it came from Alaves defender Delfi Geli whose attempted headed clearance from Gary McAllister's free kick ended up in his own net after 117 minutes. Cue the final whistle, scenes of mayhem on the terraces – and the highlight of Gerard Houllier's managerial reign. Three months after he plotted League Cup final victory against Birmingham, and just four days after the FA Cup triumph over Arsenal, Houllier had completed a Cup 'treble' that remains unique in the English game.

▼ SUCCESS AT LAST

Liverpool's first European silverware came in the shape of the UEFA Cup – a trophy they've now lifted a joint-record three times.

In 1973, when they faced Borussia Moenchengladbach, the final was still contested over two legs. The first, on a rainy May night, was abandoned after just 28 minutes because of a waterlogged Anfield pitch. But boss Bill Shankly had seen enough of the Germans' shaky central defence to convince him to change his tactics. When the match was re-staged 24 hours later, he replaced the diminutive Brian Hall with 6ft 1in John Toshack, whose aerial power caused chaos, and whose assists for Kevin Keegan led to two goals.

Centre-back Larry Lloyd added a third and, when Ray Clemence saved a penalty to preserve the vital clean sheet, Liverpool looked to have the final sewn up.

But over in Germany, they got the fright of their lives. The home side came at them with everything in the opening period, and by half-time were 2–0 up. Only heroic defending, and more superb goalkeeping from Clemence, kept them at bay after the interval. At full time, hundreds of the 4,000 Liverpool fans took to the field, in relief as much as celebration. Meanwhile, boss Bill Shankly paraded his second trophy of the season – having already delivered the League Championship for the first time in seven years. His second Anfield revolution was complete.

ABOVE: Bill Shankly and Ronnie Moran in the dug-out at the Bokelberg Stadion, 1973

LEFT: Keegan and strike partner John Toshack after clinching victory in the 1976 final against Bruges

FAR LEFT: Kevin Keegan scored in both the 1973 and 1976 UEFA Cup finals

---

UEFA CUP FINALS – LFC FIRSTS...

Manager:	Bill Shankly
Captain:	Tommy Smith
Scorer:	Kevin Keegan
Penalty-taker:	Kevin Keegan
Substitute (used):	Brian Hall

European Cup Winners

▲ BOB'S HAT-TRICK

The Reds' victory over Real Madrid in 1981 ensured Bob Paisley's name in the history books. Never before – or since – has a manager won the European Cup three times.

The triumph in Paris completed a Cup run in which they won six matches and drew three – becoming only the third team to lift the trophy without losing a single game. They owed their victory at the Parc des Princes to Alan Kennedy whose fierce 81st minute strike was enough to separate the sides. It was only the full-back's fourth goal all season, and his first appearance since breaking a wrist the previous month.

For Kirkby-born Phil Thompson it was the most memorable night of his glittering Liverpool career, as he became the first 'scouse skipper' to lift the European Cup. But amid all the wild celebrations and plaudits, the ruthless Paisley was already planning to rebuild for the future. The following season he stripped Thompson of the captaincy, and told three of his fellow finalists – David Johnson, Terry McDermott and Ray Kennedy – that they could all leave.

▼ ROME FROM HOME

25 May 1977 was the greatest night in Liverpool FC's history. The night when 13 consecutive years of continental action ended with the club taking its place among Europe's best – and when Bob Paisley's team began an era of dominance no British team has come close to matching.

The opposition: Borussia Moenchengladbach. The venue: Rome's Stadio Olimpico, awash with the red-and-white chequered flags waved by 25,000 travelling Liverpudlians. Four days earlier, many of them had been at Wembley where Manchester United ended their hopes of an historic treble by beating the Reds 2–1 in the FA Cup final. But all who made it to Rome sensed that their team were about to bury that disappointment by capturing the greatest prize of all.

ABOVE: 81st minute in '81: Alan Kennedy strikes the winner against Real Madrid in Paris

LEFT: Kevin Keegan and goalkeeper Ray Clemence were among the heroes at Rome '77

▶▶ VICTORY ON HOME SOIL

In 1978 Liverpool became the first British club to win the European Cup in consecutive seasons, and the only one to win a European trophy three years running.

This time their opponents were FC Bruges, the team they had last met in the 1976 UEFA Cup final. But whereas the Belgians had shown themselves to be attack-minded in that earlier match, they shut up shop at Wembley, packing their defence and hoping to score on the counter.

It took the Reds more than an hour to finally break them down, thanks to a sublime chip from Kenny Dalglish. It was the Scot's 30th goal in major competitions during his debut season – the most by any Liverpool player since Roger Hunt a decade earlier.

ABOVE: Kenny's clincher. Dalglish's goal in the 1978 final meant Liverpool became the first British team to retain the European Cup

▶▶ THE WOLF'S LAIR

The 1984 European Cup final was the first to be decided on penalties – and the last to be played at one of the finalist's own grounds (though it has happened in the Champions League as recently as 2012). As in 1977, Liverpool lifted the trophy at the Stadio Olimpico. But this time their opponents were Italian Champions – and full-time stadium occupants – AS Roma.

The match went to extra time after the Italians cancelled out Phil Neal's 14th minute goal just before the interval. When neither side could break the deadlock, it was time for the penalties. Steve Nicol blasted his spot-kick high and wide, becoming the first-ever player to miss from the spot in a European Cup final shoot-out. But then Bruce Grobbelaar's distraction tactics helped ensure two of the Italians were also off-target. After Neal, Graeme Souness and Ian Rush all converted, it was left to Alan Kennedy to settle matters, just as he'd done in Paris three years earlier.

Liverpool were European champions yet again – and Joe Fagan had become the first manager to win the trophy in his first season as boss.

ALRIGHT ON THE NIGHT

Terry McDermott scored Liverpool's first ever goal in a European Cup final, after 27 minutes of the 1977 clash with Borussia Moenchengladbach. After the Bundesliga champions cancelled out his effort, the Reds struck back with a brilliant, if unlikely, header from veteran Tommy Smith. Then, with eight minutes left, Kevin Keegan was hauled down in the penalty box. Phil Neal converted the spot-kick, and the 3–1 victory was sealed.

It was an emotional night for Keegan, playing his last-ever game for the club; for Paisley, who made history as the first manager to win the UEFA and European Cups in consecutive seasons; and for Emlyn Hughes, the tireless captain who played in all 62 matches during that epic campaign. As the whistle blew he became the first Liverpool skipper to lift the coveted trophy. Forty-eight hours later he showed it off to an estimated half a million fans who gathered for the city's biggest ever homecoming celebration.

RIGHT: Nice way to sign off. Graeme Souness lifts the Cup in Rome 1984. It was his last-ever match for the Reds

EUROPEAN CUP FINALS – LFC FIRSTS...

Manager:	Bob Paisley
Captain:	Emlyn Hughes
Scorer:	Terry McDermott
Penalty-taker:	Phil Neal
Substitute (used):	Steve Heighway

European Cup Winners (continued)

THE MIRACLE OF ISTANBUL

Liverpool's 2005 clash with AC Milan is widely regarded as the greatest European Cup final ever. The Reds were 3–0 down at the interval, but then staged an incredible fight-back, scoring three times in five unforgettable second half minutes.

This was the 50th European Cup final, and the first to be staged in Turkey. By going on to win the match on penalties, the Reds made history: no other team had ever overturned such a large deficit in a European Cup final. But that was just one of many records to tumble on that amazing night at the Ataturk Stadium in Istanbul.

LIVERPOOL 3–3 AC MILAN	
Gerrard (54)	Maldini (1)
Smicer (56)	Crespo (39, 44)
Alonso (59)	
Liverpool pens: Hamann, Cisse, Smicer	
Milan pens: Tomasson, Kaka	

UNITED NATIONS OF ANFIELD

Liverpool's starting XI included a Pole, a Finn, a Czech, a Norwegian, an Australian, an Irishman, a Frenchman, two Spaniards...plus Steven Gerrard and Jamie Carragher. Never before has a winning team included so few players from its home nation. A third Englishman – Scott Carson – was on the bench but not used. Other subs included two Spaniards, a Croatian, a Czech, a Frenchman and a German.

FASTEST AND OLDEST

Milan's opener came after just 51 seconds – the fastest-ever goal in a European Cup final. Veteran full-back Paolo Maldini struck home a 12-yard volley to become – at 36 – the oldest player to score in the final.

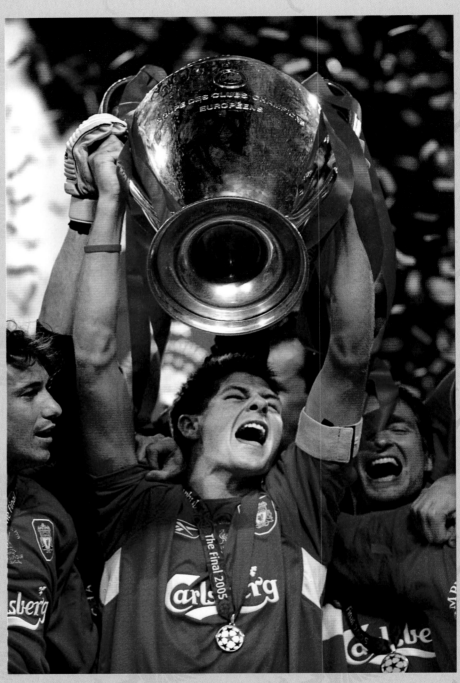

ABOVE: Turkish delight. Skipper Steven Gerrard hoists Liverpool's fifth European Cup after the most unlikely of victories in Istanbul

TRAVELLING KOPITES, TAKE A BOW

Although Liverpool's official ticket allocation was 20,000, the true number of Reds fans inside the stadium was estimated to be between 35,000 and 40,000. If so, it was the greatest number of supporters to follow the team from one country to another. The Liverpool fans – already noted for their noise and passion – won worldwide admiration for their incredible show of loyalty at half-time. With their team 3–0 down, they struck up a deafening rendition of 'You'll Never Walk Alone'.

POLE IN THE GOAL

Although Steven Gerrard won the 'Man of the Match' accolade, victory wouldn't have been possible without Jerzy Dudek's heroics in goal. His incredible 'double save' from Andriy Shevchenko in the last minute of extra time – later voted the 'Most Memorable Champions League Moment' – ensured the game went to penalties. Once it did, he emulated Bruce Grobbelaar's antics in the 1984 final by wobbling his legs in an attempt to distract the Milan penalty-takers. The tactic worked. Dudek saved two spot-kicks, with the last one from Shevchenko sealing victory.

RAFA'S DOUBLE

In guiding Liverpool to victory, Rafa Benitez equalled Joe Fagan's feat of winning the trophy in his first season in charge at Anfield. He also matched Bob Paisley's achievement of lifting the UEFA Cup and the European Cup in consecutive campaigns. A year before the Istanbul triumph he had led Valencia to a 2–0 victory over Marseilles.

OURS FOR KEEPS

Under UEFA rules any club that won the European Cup five times in total – or three times in a row – was allowed to keep the trophy, while the governing body commissioned a new one to be competed for in subsequent seasons. Liverpool joined Real Madrid, Ajax, Bayern Munich and Milan in being able to put the trophy on permanent display in their trophy cabinet. But they are the last to enjoy the privilege. In 2009 UEFA decided that it should retain the original, and produce a full-size replica for each season's winners.

GOALS GALORE

This was the highest-scoring final of the Champions League era, and had more goals than any final since 1962 – the year Benfica beat Real Madrid 5–3. Amazingly, all the goals – both from open play, and in the shoot-out – were scored at the same end. It was behind this goal that the Milan fans were congregated.

SPOT-KICK KINGS

In replicating their shoot-out victory over Roma in 1984, the Reds became the first team to win two European Cup finals on penalties. Although John Arne Riise missed from the spot, Didi Hamann, Djibril Cisse and Vladimir Smicer all converted. Hamann scored despite having broken a toe. Smicer, who had earlier scored Liverpool's second goal from open play, never appeared for the club again.

RHAPSODY IN RED

The final against Milan came nearly 41 years after a European Cup tie against Anderlecht, when Bill Shankly sent his team out in an all-red kit for the first time. They wore those same colours in Istanbul, just as they did in the other four finals they won. On each occasion the opposition were in all-white.

TIME'S UP

Although the shoot-out was over after nine penalties instead of the full 10, it didn't finish until after midnight. That meant the match – which kicked off at 9.45pm Istanbul time, actually stretched across two days.

BELOW: The homecoming. Thousands of fans celebrate outside the city's St. George's Hall awaiting their heroes' return

Liverpool Player Records

More than 700 names have appeared on Liverpool team-sheets since the club was formed in 1892. The first side to take to the field included 10 Scots and one Englishman – the so-called 'Team of the Macs', recruited by LFC's original manager, John McKenna.

Records were set from the off. The opening fixture was the only game in which 11 Liverpool players made their debuts. The following month they played their first home FA Cup tie, securing a 9–0 victory over Newtown, which remains the highest win in the tournament at Anfield. Just a few weeks later prolific striker John Miller lined up in the 7–0 win over Fleetwood Rangers, becoming the first Liverpool player to score five goals in one match.

Countless records have been made, and broken, by the successors of that original Liverpool team, and every season brings new milestones. In 2012–13 Steven Gerrard became the first Liverpool player to win 100 England caps, and reached an unprecedented European goals total of 39. Jamie Carragher ended his career as the only player to serve under six different managers at Anfield. And in the same season a veteran defender made his last appearance, a teenage striker made his first: at 16 years and six days, Jerome Sinclair became the youngest Liverpool player ever.

Few records are permanent. But, for a time, they are all unique. These are the players who have made history with LFC.

RIGHT: End of an era. Jamie Carragher made his 508th and final appearance for the Reds in 2012–13

BELOW: The Liverpool squad ahead of the 1977–78 season – a year that saw the Reds retain the European Cup

Appearances

Players and fans have always had a special bond at Anfield. Those on the terraces give their whole-hearted support – while those on the pitch give every ounce of effort. Appearing for Liverpool brings fame ands wealth, but also responsibility. 'The supporters will never achieve their dream because they can't play,' says Kenny Dalglish. 'So they live their dream through us.'

 ### CALLY – BUILT TO LAST

With 857 appearances, Ian Callaghan has played more games for Liverpool than anyone else. He also tops the chart for League appearances, playing in 640 matches. The club was in Division Two obscurity when he made his teenage debut. By the time he left in 1978, the Reds were the Champions of Europe.

'Cally' took the place of his idol Billy Liddell in 1960, and went on to surpass the Scotsman's record of 534 appearances in all competitions. Fourteen years after making his debut he became the first LFC player to win the Footballer of the Year accolade, and collected an MBE for his services to the game.

By then he was 32 and considered by many to be a veteran who was close to retirement. Yet some of his greatest achievements were still ahead of him. He played in all but two fixtures in the 1975–76 campaign, when Liverpool won a Championship and UEFA Cup double. He then made 48 appearances the following season to help land both the League title and European Cup. Just a few months later he was recalled to the England team – 11 years after his last international appearance.

 ### SPANNING THE YEARS

Alan Hansen was the first outfield player in the English game to collect League Championship medals in three different decades. He picked up his first in 1979, two years after making his Liverpool debut. He collected his eighth in 1990, by which time he had made 620 appearances for the club in all competitions.

GREAT SCOTT

Goalkeeper Elisha Scott holds the record for the longest first-team career at Anfield. He made his debut against Newcastle on New Year's Day 1913, and played his last match against Chelsea 21 years and 52 days later. The legendary Ulsterman carried on playing after leaving Liverpool, making his last international appearance at the age of 42.

MOST APPEARANCES – ALL COMPETITIONS	
Ian Callaghan	857
Jamie Carragher	737
Ray Clemence	665
Emlyn Hughes	665
Ian Rush	660
Phil Neal	650
Tommy Smith	638
Steven Gerrard	630
Bruce Grobbelaar	628
Alan Hansen	620

ABOVE RIGHT: Alan Hansen tasted League Championship success in three different decades

RIGHT: With 857, Ian Callaghan made more appearances than any other Liverpool player

▶▶ BOYS TO MEN

Jerome Sinclair's substitute appearance in a 2012 League Cup tie at West Bromwich Albion made him the youngest player to turn out for the Reds. At just 16 years and six days, he beat the record set by Jack Robinson, who made his debut in 2010 at 16 years, 250 days.

Goalkeeper Ned Doig is the oldest player, making his last appearance in 1908 when he was 41 years, 165 days old. Doig, who signed from Sunderland, is also the oldest debutant, playing his first game on the opening day of the 1904–05 season, aged 37 years, 307 days.

▼ WHAT DO YOU MEAN, 'ROTATION'?

Full-back Phil Neal played an incredible 417 consecutive matches between October 1976 and September 1983 – an achievement that won't be beaten for many years to come. He also holds the record for most seasons as an ever-present, turning out for every game in eight different campaigns. His run coincided with a period of unparalleled success, when the team were routinely playing more than 60 matches per season. His determination was as staggering as his stamina: he played on through illness and injuries, including a fractured cheekbone

and a broken toe. Neal was superb in attack as well as defence, scoring 59 times in his 650 appearances. For several years, he was also the first-choice penalty-taker, whose spot kick in Rome helped seal the Reds' first-ever European Cup triumph in 1977. Seven years later he converted another penalty in the final shoot-out against AS Roma, to add to his earlier goal from open play.

ABOVE: A bright future ahead. Jerome Sinclair is the youngest-ever player to turn out for Liverpool

BELOW: 'Mr Dependable' Phil Neal played in every game for eight successive seasons

NO SHIFTING THEM

Under the modern squad system it's rare for even first-choice players to appear in every game during a season. Jose Reina and Martin Skrtel played in all 38 Premier League matches in 2010–11, but were both rested for early cup ties. The last players to go through the entire fixture list were David James and Stig Inge Bjornebye – and that was in 1996–97. In 1965–66, LFC had a record number of ever-presents, with Tommy Lawrence, Gerry Byrne, Ron Yeats, Tommy Smith and Ian Callaghan playing in all 53 domestic and European matches.

MOST SEASONS AS AN EVER-PRESENT

Phil Neal	8
Chris Lawler	6
Ian Callaghan	5
Ray Clemence	5
Bruce Grobbelaar	5

MOST LEAGUE APPEARANCES

Ian Callaghan	640
Jamie Carragher	508
Billy Liddell	492
Emlyn Hughes	474
Ray Clemence	470
Ian Rush	469
Tommy Smith	467
Phil Neal	455
Bruce Grobbelaar	440
Steven Gerrard	440
Alan Hansen	434

► CARRY ON CARRA

The UEFA Europa League tie against Zenit St. Petersburg in February 2013 marked Jamie Carragher's 150th and final appearance in European competitions. No other Liverpool player has faced continental opposition as many times, or in as many seasons. After making his UEFA Cup debut against Celtic at Anfield in 1997, Carragher competed in Europe during 14 different campaigns – a record only equalled by Ian Callaghan. The Bootle-born defender's run of games included 91 Champions League ties, 29 in the Europa League, 28 in the UEFA Cup and two in the European Super Cup. In addition he played twice in the FIFA Club World Championship.

▼ MEN FOR THE BIG OCCASION

Phil Neal holds the club record for appearances in European finals. After finishing his first full season as part of the 1976 UEFA Cup-winning side, he was in the line-ups for all four European Cup triumphs under Bob Paisley and Joe Fagan. He was captain for his sixth final, played amid the tragedy of Heysel. Ray Clemence played in five European finals, and was victorious in them all. When the Reds clinched their third European Cup in Paris in 1981, he was the only surviving member of the 1973 UEFA Cup-winning team. It was his 665th and last game for the club – a record for a goalkeeper.

SWEET FA SUCCESS

Tommy Smith and Ian Callaghan set new club records against Manchester United at Wembley in 1977, becoming the first to appear in four FA Cup finals – an achievement later equalled by Bruce Grobbelaar, Steve Nicol and Ian Rush. Both Smith and Callaghan were on the losing side that day, although they did pick up winner's medals on their first Wembley appearances in 1965, and again in 1974. Callaghan took part in the tournament during 17 seasons, making a record 79 appearances for the club.

BELOW: No 1 on the continent. Clemence played in five European finals while with Liverpool

BELOW: Well-travelled. Jamie Carragher holds the club record for most European appearances

MOST EUROPEAN APPEARANCES

Jamie Carragher	150
Steven Gerrard	124
Sami Hyypia	94
Ian Callaghan	89
Tommy Smith	85
Jose Reina	84
Ray Clemence	80
Emlyn Hughes	79
John Arne Riise	79
Phil Neal	74

PAISLEY SNUBBED

The FA Cup remained famously absent from manager Bob Paisley's trophy cabinet – and it was an unhappy competition for him as a player, too. He was the hero of the 1950 semi-final, scoring the first in a 2–0 win against Everton at Maine Road. But a month later, when the team faced Arsenal at Wembley, he was dropped. Paisley was said to be 'shattered' by the decision and even considered quitting Anfield. Thankfully, his friend and team-mate Albert Stubbins persuaded him to stay.

FOREIGN LEGION

Liverpool made history in the 1986 Wembley clash with Everton, fielding an FA Cup final side without a single Englishman. The team included four Scots (Steve Nicol, Alan Hansen, Kenny Dalglish and Kevin MacDonald), three Irishmen (Jim Beglin, Mark Lawrenson and Ronnie Whelan), one Welshman (Ian Rush), a Zimbabwean (Bruce Grobbelaar), a South African (Craig Johnston) and a Dane (Jan Molby). The Liverpool-born substitute Steve McMahon was unused.

STERLING JOB

Raheem Sterling is the youngest Liverpool player to take part in an FA Cup match. His appearance in the Fourth Round tie against Oldham Athletic in January 2013 came when he was 18 years and 50 days old – 157 days younger than Barry Wilkinson who had held the record since 1954.

▶▶ OLD HEADS

At 40 years and 116 days, Elisha Scott is the oldest Reds player to feature in the FA Cup. The veteran keeper set the record in a Fifth Round home tie against Bolton in 1934. Sixty-seven years later, Gary McAllister became the oldest to appear in an FA Cup final, coming on as a substitute against Arsenal at Cardiff's Millennium Stadium aged 36 years and 137 days.

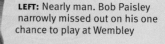

LEFT: Nearly man. Bob Paisley narrowly missed out on his one chance to play at Wembley

RUSHIE'S CUP

Liverpool's long wait for success in the League Cup coincided with Ian Rush's arrival in the first-team. It was a tournament the striker would make his own throughout his career. He not only set a new joint record for goals in the competition, he played in more games, lined up in more finals, and collected more winner's medals than any player before or since. In total, he made 78 appearances, scored 48 goals, and was on the winning side in five out of six finals.

SIX OF THE BEST

When the Reds won back to back League Cups between 1981 and 1984, Ian Rush was one of six players to appear in all four successive finals. The other five were Phil Neal, Alan Kennedy, Alan Hansen, Kenny Dalglish and Sammy Lee.

BELOW: Sammy Lee was one of six Liverpool players to appear in four successive League Cup finals between 1981 and 1984

MOST FA CUP APPEARANCES

Ian Callaghan	79
Bruce Grobbelaar	62
Emlyn Hughes	62
Ian Rush	61
Alan Hansen	58
Ray Clemence	54
Tommy Smith	52
John Barnes	51
Ron Yeats	50
Steve Nicol	50

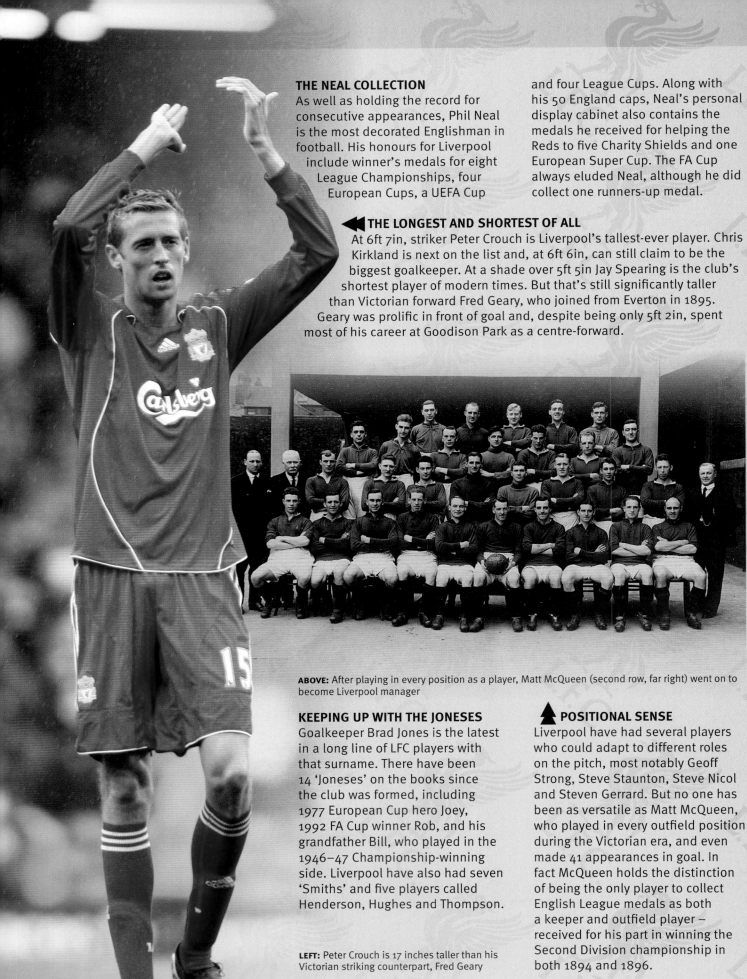

THE NEAL COLLECTION

As well as holding the record for consecutive appearances, Phil Neal is the most decorated Englishman in football. His honours for Liverpool include winner's medals for eight League Championships, four European Cups, a UEFA Cup and four League Cups. Along with his 50 England caps, Neal's personal display cabinet also contains the medals he received for helping the Reds to five Charity Shields and one European Super Cup. The FA Cup always eluded Neal, although he did collect one runners-up medal.

◄ THE LONGEST AND SHORTEST OF ALL

At 6ft 7in, striker Peter Crouch is Liverpool's tallest-ever player. Chris Kirkland is next on the list and, at 6ft 6in, can still claim to be the biggest goalkeeper. At a shade over 5ft 5in Jay Spearing is the club's shortest player of modern times. But that's still significantly taller than Victorian forward Fred Geary, who joined from Everton in 1895. Geary was prolific in front of goal and, despite being only 5ft 2in, spent most of his career at Goodison Park as a centre-forward.

ABOVE: After playing in every position as a player, Matt McQueen (second row, far right) went on to become Liverpool manager

KEEPING UP WITH THE JONESES

Goalkeeper Brad Jones is the latest in a long line of LFC players with that surname. There have been 14 'Joneses' on the books since the club was formed, including 1977 European Cup hero Joey, 1992 FA Cup winner Rob, and his grandfather Bill, who played in the 1946–47 Championship-winning side. Liverpool have also had seven 'Smiths' and five players called Henderson, Hughes and Thompson.

LEFT: Peter Crouch is 17 inches taller than his Victorian striking counterpart, Fred Geary

▲ POSITIONAL SENSE

Liverpool have had several players who could adapt to different roles on the pitch, most notably Geoff Strong, Steve Staunton, Steve Nicol and Steven Gerrard. But no one has been as versatile as Matt McQueen, who played in every outfield position during the Victorian era, and even made 41 appearances in goal. In fact McQueen holds the distinction of being the only player to collect English League medals as both a keeper and outfield player – received for his part in winning the Second Division championship in both 1894 and 1896.

▶▶ RELATIVE VALUES

Dean Saunders was a record signing when he arrived at Liverpool for £2.9 million in 1991. He was also the first man to follow in his father's footsteps by playing for the club. His dad Roy, also a Welsh international, spent six seasons at Anfield during the 1950s, making 146 appearances, compared to Dean's 61 games.

Eleven years after captain Paul Ince left, his son Tom also got his Liverpool first-team chance. However, he was limited to just one appearance off the bench in the 2010–11 season before moving to Blackpool.

Joe Fagan spent 27 years at Anfield as trainer, first-team coach and manager. However, his days as a player were spent at Manchester City and Bradford Park Avenue. His son Chris does figure in LFC playing history, making two appearances as a full-back in the 1969–70 season.

▼ PRODIGAL SONS

Craig Bellamy was the most recent of only six players who've had two spells at Anfield. The Welshman re-signed in 2011, four years after leaving for West Ham.

RIGHT: Doing his dad proud. Dean Saunders followed in father Roy's footsteps

BELOW: Nice to be back. Craig Bellamy enjoyed two spells at the club

PLAYERS WITH TWO SPELLS AT LIVERPOOL FC

Player	Joined	Left	Re-signed
George Allan	1895	1897	1898
Alf West	1903	1909	1910
Ian Rush	1980	1987	1988
Steve Staunton	1986	1991	1998
Robbie Fowler	1991	2001	2006
Craig Bellamy	2006	2007	2011

GUEST PLAYERS

In matches staged during World War II, the Football League allowed clubs to field players from other teams if their Army or RAF bases were nearby. Among the dozens of players who guested for Liverpool between 1939 and 1945 was Don Welsh. The Charlton Athletic forward, who would later manage LFC, scored 44 times in 39 games – including six in a 12–1 victory over Southport.

In May 1942, another future boss made his one and only guest appearance. When the Reds took on Everton in a wartime friendly at Anfield, the man wearing the No. 4 shirt was Preston North End's Bill Shankly.

THE SEVEN-YEAR HITCH

Cyril Done scored Liverpool's winner on his League debut against Chelsea in September 1939 – but then had to wait another seven years for his next senior match. The reason? The outbreak of World War II led to the suspension of the Football League programme. When the Bootle-born striker did re-appear, in a Division One game against Charlton in October 1946, he was again on the scoresheet in a 1–1 draw. Done therefore has the longest gap between debut and second appearance in LFC player history. However, it doesn't appear in the official statistics, as the Football Association later expunged the three games played at the start of the 1939–40 season from their records.

Goalscoring

Liverpool have scored 9,235 goals in competitive matches since the club was formed – the last coming from Phillipe Coutinho on the last day of the 2012–13 season. The Reds have scored 471 penalties, and found the net an average of 1.7 times per match. More than 400 names appear on the Liverpool scoring list, including some of the finest strikers the world has ever seen.

BELOW: Simply the best. Ian Rush is Liverpool's all-time record goalscorer

▶ GOAL RUSH

Ian Rush is the most prolific striker to play for Liverpool in any era. The Welshman broke almost every conceivable scoring record during his two spells at Anfield. Nearly two decades after leaving, his overall goals tally of 346 is still streets ahead of his nearest rival.

Rush's 47 goals in all competitions in the 1983–84 season remains unsurpassed by anyone at the club. As does his record of 25 goals in Merseyside derbies, along with his 39 in the FA Cup and 48 in the League Cup. Only Liverpool's enforced absence from continental competition after the Heysel disaster

prevented him from adding to his total of 20 goals in Europe. However, he continued to leave his mark on the international stage, becoming the most prolific-ever striker for the Welsh national side, with 28 goals.

Rush broke Roger Hunt's all-time scoring record with a goal in the Reds' 2–2 Premiership draw with Manchester United at Old Trafford in 1992. Earlier that year, he wrote his name into FA Cup history when he scored the second in the 2–0 victory over Sunderland at Wembley. That gave him five goals in FA Cup finals – more than any player in the tournament's history.

ALL-TIME TOP SCORERS

Ian Rush	346
Roger Hunt	286
Gordon Hodgson	241
Billy Liddell	228
Robbie Fowler	183
Kenny Dalglish	172
Steven Gerrard	159
Michael Owen	158
Harry Chambers	151
Sam Raybould	130

BELOW: Early scorers: John Smith (front row, second left), Malcolm McVean (front row, second right), and James McBride (second row, second right)

J. McQue.   J McCartney.   A. Hannah.   S. H. Ross.   M. McQueen.   D. McLean.   J. McBride   A. Dick (*Trainer*).
T. Wyllie.   J. Smith.   J. Miller.   M. McVean.   H. McQueen.

◀ FIRST ON THE SCORESHEET

On 3 September 1892, John Smith opened the scoring in Liverpool's inaugural Lancashire League fixture against Higher Walton. The 25-year-old Scottish forward began an 8–0 rout, and secured his name in the record books as the scorer of the club's first competitive goal. Two days earlier, the team played their first-ever match: a friendly against Rotherham Town at Anfield, where Malcolm McVean hit the opener in a 7–1 win.

McVean also scored LFC's first ever League goal in a 2–0 Second Division victory over Middlesbrough Ironopolis on 2 September 1893. One week later, James McBride scored Liverpool's first league goal at Anfield in a 4–0 win against Lincoln City.

BLINK AND YOU'LL MISS IT

It took Liverpool-born striker Jack Balmer just 10 seconds to find the net in the 1937–38 League derby at Goodison Park – a match the Reds went on to win 3–1 in front of 33,465 spectators. It was, according to one newspaper report 'a sensational opening...hardly an Everton player touched the ball'. In September 1985, Kenny Dalglish opened the scoring in the same fixture – after only 20 seconds!

Balmer's goal remains the fastest recorded in Liverpool's history. The quickest goal scored in European competition came at Anfield on 16 September 2010, when Joe Cole was on target against Steaua Bucharest after 26 seconds.

LEFT: Quick-fire striker. Jack Balmer's goal against Everton was the fastest-ever for the club

THEY'RE QUEUEING UP...

When Brazilian Philippe Coutinho struck the second goal in a 5–0 victory over Swansea in February 2013 he became the 18th different Liverpool player to score in League and Cup matches during one season – equalling the record set in 1999–2000.

The most players to get on the scoresheet in a single match is nine. Phil Boersma and Phil Thompson both netted twice in the 11–0 rout of Stromsgodset in 1974, while Alec Lindsay, Steve Heighway, Peter Cormack, Emlyn Hughes, Tommy Smith, Ian Callaghan and Ray Kennedy all added one each. Brian Hall was the only outfield player who failed to get a goal against the Norwegian part-timers.

WHAM BAM, THANK YOU SAM

Sam Raybould was the first Liverpool striker to hit 100 goals. Almost a century after his last appearance, he still appears on the all-time Top 10 scorers' list, with a tally of 130. The Derbyshire-born striker joined the Reds in 1900, and helped them to win their first League Championship the following season with 17 goals. He was also on target 11 times in the 1905–06 title-winning campaign. But his most prolific season was in 1902–03, when he struck 32 goals in just 34 league and FA Cup appearances.

FIVE GO MAD... IN FRONT OF GOAL

When Robbie Fowler scored all Liverpool's goals in a 5–0 League Cup tie against Fulham in 1993, he joined one of the most select band of strikers in the club's history. Only five LFC players have ever scored as many times in one match, and Fowler, at just 18, was the youngest. Twenty-three Reds' strikers have hit the target four times in a single match. Both Fowler and Michael Owen did it twice, while Ian Rush achieved the feat three times.

LIVERPOOL PLAYERS WHO'VE SCORED FIVE IN ONE MATCH

John Miller (v Fleetwood Rangers, 1892)
Andy McGuigan (v Stoke City, 1902)
Johnny Evans (v Bristol Rovers, 1954)
Ian Rush (v Luton Town, 1983)
Robbie Fowler (v Fulham, 1993)

LEFT: High-five. Robbie Fowler was still a teenager when he went nap in a League Cup tie against Fulham at Anfield in 1993

A LEAGUE OF HIS OWN

Roger Hunt may only have been awarded an MBE for his services to football, but to Liverpool fans he'll forever be known as 'Sir'. Ian Rush later overtook him as the club's overall top scorer but, with 245 goals in 404 Division One and Two matches, his League record remains intact. As does his feat of scoring 41 goals in as many appearances in the 1961–62 promotion winning campaign: the most any Liverpool player has scored in the League in a single season.

After scoring on his debut against Scunthorpe in 1959, Hunt struck up a productive partnership with fellow striker Dave Hickson, but really hit his stride when Ian St. John arrived to join him in attack. From 1962 to 1969 he was the club's leading marksman, using his physical strength, speed and ferocious shot to terrorise opposition defences. His goals were largely responsible for delivering Bill Shankly his first two Championship titles. But as well as his exploits in the League, Hunt will also be remembered as the first ever Liverpool player to score in an FA Cup final.

ABOVE: A sign of the times. Youngsters collect Roger Hunt's autograph before a 1960s match at Anfield.

RIGHT: John Aldridge was a goal-machine for Liverpool in the 1987–88 season

ALDO'S PERFECT 10

Liverpool's flying start to the 1987–88 Division One season was due to a combination of skill, free-flowing football – and a relentless goalscoring machine named John Aldridge. The local-born striker, bought to replace the Juventus-bound Ian Rush, was on target in each of the Reds' opening nine League fixtures, grabbing 11 of their 28 goals. But his record-breaking sequence stretched back even further. As he'd netted on the closing day of the previous season, 'Aldo' became the only Liverpool player to score in 10 consecutive League matches.

The striker made his final appearance in September 1989, coming on as a substitute and immediately scoring a penalty to help his side demolish Crystal Palace 9–0 at Anfield. With 63 goals in 104 appearances he had scored more per game than any Liverpool player in more than half a century.

ROBBIE'S SUPER-FAST CENTURIES

Robbie Fowler took just 165 matches to hit 100 goals in all competitions – beating Ian Rush's record by one game. He reached the milestone in style, scoring after just 29 seconds, then adding three more in a 5–1 victory over Middlesbrough in December 1996. He celebrated by unveiling a T-shirt with the words 'Job's A Good 'Un' scrawled across his chest.

He completed his League century in 175 games, making him the fourth fastest player in Premiership history to reach 100 goals. The match in January 1999 was another one to remember as Liverpool thumped Southampton 7–1 at Anfield, and Fowler weighed in with a hat-trick. By the time Robbie finished his second spell at Anfield in 2007, he had scored 183 goals for the Reds including 128 in the Premier League.

WONDER START FOR 'EL NINO'

Fernando Torres is the fastest-ever Liverpool player to hit 50 League goals. His milestone strike came in the 90th minute at Villa Park in December 2009 – in only his 72nd Premier League outing for the club.

Torres' early impact on the English game was sensational. After starting with an Anfield debut goal against Chelsea in the League, his scoring run included three hat-tricks and a sequence of eight home matches in which he found the net every time. While on the way to breaking the League record he also weighed in with eight Champions League goals, three more in the League Cup and one in the FA Cup.

BEST GOALS-TO-GAMES RATIO

Three LFC players can boast a goal for every senior game played – then again, they all made just one appearance each! They were Ben Bull in 1896, John Sealey in 1965 and Layton Maxwell in a 4–2 Worthington Cup victory over Hull City at Anfield in September 1999.

But even their goals-to-games ratio isn't as impressive as that of the club's original star striker, John Miller, who found the net 23 times in 22 games during the club's inaugural campaign in the Lancashire League. He also added three in as many FA Cup ties before leaving the club at the end of that season – with his Anfield career statistics showing 26 goals in 25 games.

RIGHT: Fernando Torres in full flow during his first season at Anfield

MICHAEL THE WONDERKID

At 17 years and 144 days old, Michael Owen is the youngest goalscorer in the club's history. His strike came on his 1997 debut against Wimbledon at Selhurst Park, more than four decades after scouser Jimmy Melia got on the first-team scoresheet, at just 18 years and 46 days. (Melia remained the club's second youngest scorer until October 2012, when Raheem Sterling – then 17 years, 312 days old – grabbed the only goal in the 1–0 Premier League victory over Reading at Anfield.)

Owen's goal in the penultimate match of the Premiership season was just a small sign of things to come. He finished the following campaign as the Premiership's joint leading scorer with 18 League goals, and became – at 18 years and 59 days – the youngest England player of the 20th century.

RIGHT: Michael Owen was a prolific teenaged goalscorer for both club and country

STEVIE WONDER

Steven Gerrard comfortably tops Liverpool's European scoring chart with 39 goals – 17 ahead of his nearest rival, Michael Owen. The Reds skipper opened his account with a header in the November 2000 UEFA Cup tie against Greek side Olympiacos. Six months later, in the final of the same competition, he was on the scoresheet again, hitting Liverpool's second in an epic 5–4 victory over Alaves of Spain.

In May 2005, Gerrard inspired his side to the greatest European fight-back of all-time, heading their first goal as they came from 3–0 down to beat AC Milan in the Champions League final in Istanbul. His exploits in both European and domestic knock-out tournaments have brought him another unique record. He is the only player to have scored in the finals of the FA Cup, League Cup, European Cup and UEFA Cup.

RED HOT IN ICELAND

Long before Steven Gerrard began terrorising continental defences, Liverpool took their first tentative steps in Europe. In 1964 they went into the European Cup for the first

ABOVE: Ahead of the rest. Steven Gerrard's goal in Istanbul was one of 39 in European competitions

BELOW: Never too old. Gary McAllister was on target in the 2001 UEFA Cup final

time, and found themselves drawn against the Icelandic champions, Reykjavik, in the qualifying rounds. It was a journey into the unknown for the Reds, but they needn't have worried. By the end of the first leg they were 5–0 up against the part-timers, with inside-forward Gordon Wallace setting them on their way with a goal after just three minutes. The Scot had been drafted in to replace regular striker Ian St. John who was recovering from appendicitis. He was absent from the 6–1 second-leg win, when left-back Gerry Byrne treated Reds' fans to Anfield's first European goal.

GOLDEN OLDIES

By 1960, Billy Liddell's career was drawing to a close. But the legendary winger, who broke records galore during his time at Anfield, still had one more reason to put his name in the history books. On 5 March that year, he hit the third in a 5–1 home win over Stoke City, making him – at 38 years, 55 days – Liverpool's oldest marksman.

Gary McAllister is the club's most senior European scorer, thanks to his goal in the 2001 UEFA Cup final against Alaves at the age of 36 years, 141 days. Two weeks earlier his goal against Bradford City made him the club's oldest Premiership scorer, at 36 years, 126 days.

KING BOTH SIDES OF THE BORDER

When Kenny Dalglish scored against Exeter City in an October 1981 League Cup tie he became the only Liverpool player to hit a century of goals in different countries. Dalglish joined the Reds after a glittering eight years at Celtic, where he was on target 112 times in 204 appearances. During an even more successful career at Anfield he scored 172 goals, with 118 of them in the League.

Dalglish was on target in each of his first four appearances in his debut 1977–78 season. He ended the campaign as top scorer with 31 goals, and crowned his magnificent first year by scoring the winner in the European Cup final against FC Bruges at Wembley.

▼ OFF TO A FLYER

In January 2013, Daniel Sturridge became the 89th player to score on his Liverpool debut with an opening strike against Mansfield Town in the FA Cup Third Round. Others on target in their first appearance include Billy Liddell, Roger Hunt, Kevin Keegan, Ray Kennedy, Robbie Fowler, Michael Owen and Luis Suarez.

In 1993 Nigel Clough hit a double against Sheffield Wednesday, becoming the first Liverpool player to score twice on his debut since Dave Hickson back in 1959. No Reds player has ever scored three in their opening competitive game. Bobby Graham got a hat-trick on his League debut in 1964, but he'd made his first appearance in a European tie against Reykjavik 12 days earlier – a match in which he also scored.

BELOW: Dan's the man. Sturridge gets off the mark on his debut against Mansfield Town in the FA Cup

LAST TEN PLAYERS TO SCORE ON DEBUT

Daniel Sturridge	Mark Gonzalez
Andre Wisdom	Abel Xavier
Luis Suarez	Layton Maxwell
Gabriel Paletta	Titi Camara
Craig Bellamy	Michael Owen

▲ THAT'S WHY THEY CALLED HIM 'SUPERSUB'

With 18 goals as a substitute, David Fairclough has made a bigger impact than any other Liverpool player when coming off the bench. The flame-haired striker's goals helped Bob Paisley achieve unprecedented success both at home and in Europe, but throughout his eight years at Anfield he struggled to command a regular starting place. Fast, skilful and possessing a powerful shot,

▶▶ ALONSO FROM AFAR

Xabi Alonso's unforgettable 70-yard strike in the 2–0 Premier League win against Newcastle in September 2006 was described by the *Independent* newspaper as "one of the most audacious goals in Anfield's rich 115-year history". It was also believed to be the furthest. The match was 78 minutes old when the Spaniard broke up an opposition attack midway inside his own half, then, spotting Newcastle keeper Steve Harper off his line, hit a perfectly weighted right-footer that began life just outside the centre circle, and ended in the back of the Kop net.

Fairclough would have walked into the first team of any other club in the world during the 1970s. But at Liverpool he came of age in the era of Keegan, Toshack and Heighway; then matured as Johnson, Dalglish and Rush were at their most deadly.

Such competition for places meant he was usually overlooked when it came to team selection. But his ability to turn a game meant he was often more valuable coming on midway through the

Incredibly, it was the second time in eight months that Alonso scored from inside his own half – the first coming in a third-round FA Cup victory at Luton. That strike led to one Reds fan collecting £25,000 in winnings after betting on Alonso to score from Liverpool territory at some stage of the 2005–06 season.

ABOVE: Twelfth man. David Fairclough scores his unforgettable winner against St. Etienne

RIGHT: Not too Xabi! Alonso hit the target from 70 yards

second half, his fresh legs running opposition defences ragged. This was demonstrated most effectively towards the end of the 1975–76 season, when he scored seven times in eight appearances – six as substitute – to tip the chase for the League title in his team's favour. One year on, his dramatic match-winning intervention in the European Cup quarter-final against St. Etienne forever ensured his place in LFC folklore.

TOP GOALSCORING SUBS

1	David Fairclough	18
2	Ryan Babbel	12
3	Steven Gerrard	8
4	Djibril Cisse	7
5	Ian Rush	6
=	Michael Owen	6
=	Vladimir Smicer	6
8	Robbie Fowler	5
=	Emile Heskey	5
=	David Johnson	5
=	Luis Suarez	5

▶▶ DIRK'S LATE, LATE SHOW

Dirk Kuyt's penalty at the Emirates Stadium on 17 April 2011, was the latest recorded goal in a Football League or Premier League match for 123 years. Referee Andre Marriner had added on eight minutes to compensate for Jamie Carragher's concussion earlier in the game, which stood at 0–0 at the end of normal time. At 90+8, Liverpool conceded a penalty, duly slotted home by Robin Van Persie. But as the home fans celebrated what looked like certain victory, Marriner added yet more time to make up for further delays, then blew for a foul on Lucas Leiva in Arsenal's penalty area. Kuyt's immaculately placed spot kick was officially timed at 90+11mins 48secs. Just eight seconds later, the final whistle was blown.

ABOVE: Over and Kuyt. Dirk slots home the latest-ever winner in an English league match

DEJA VU

Robbie Fowler scored many special goals for Liverpool, but few were as memorable as his 90th-minute strike to beat Newcastle United at Anfield on 10 March 1997. He completed a double to give the Reds a second consecutive 4–3 Premiership victory over the Magpies. Amazingly, on 3 April 1996, Fowler had also scored twice in the victory, and Stan Collymore had scored in the dying seconds to win a pulsating encounter.

STOPPING THE OPPOSITION WAS MORE IMPORTANT

Stephane Henchoz and Rob Jones were terrific defenders, but will hardly be remembered for their abilities in front of the opposition goal. With 205 and 243 games respectively, neither managed a single effort on target. Still, their scoring records are better than that of Ephraim Longworth, who played 370 games between 1910 and 1928, and didn't get on the scoresheet once.

RIGHT: Birthday boy. Ronnie Whelan came of age with two goals against Southampton

◀◀ GOOD REASON TO CELEBRATE

Phil Thompson, Steve McManaman, Terry McDermott, Peter Crouch and Andy Carroll are just a few of the LFC players to get on the scoresheet on their birthdays. Both Robbie Fowler and Ronnie Whelan were on target the same day they turned 21, with the Irishman hitting a double in a 5–0 win against Southampton. But the man with greatest reason to break out the champagne was Geordie striker Bobby Robinson, whose four goals against Leicester Fosse sent the Reds to the top of Division One on 1 October 1904 – his 25th birthday.

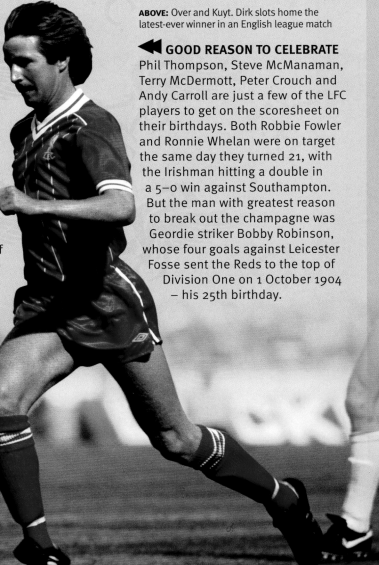

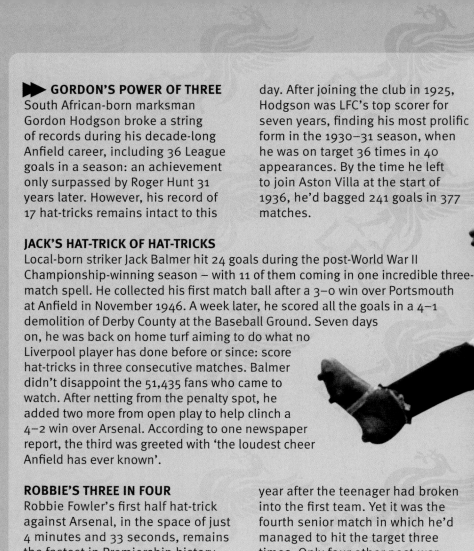

GORDON'S POWER OF THREE

South African-born marksman Gordon Hodgson broke a string of records during his decade-long Anfield career, including 36 League goals in a season: an achievement only surpassed by Roger Hunt 31 years later. However, his record of 17 hat-tricks remains intact to this day. After joining the club in 1925, Hodgson was LFC's top scorer for seven years, finding his most prolific form in the 1930–31 season, when he was on target 36 times in 40 appearances. By the time he left to join Aston Villa at the start of 1936, he'd bagged 241 goals in 377 matches.

JACK'S HAT-TRICK OF HAT-TRICKS

Local-born striker Jack Balmer hit 24 goals during the post-World War II Championship-winning season – with 11 of them coming in one incredible three-match spell. He collected his first match ball after a 3–0 win over Portsmouth at Anfield in November 1946. A week later, he scored all the goals in a 4–1 demolition of Derby County at the Baseball Ground. Seven days on, he was back on home turf aiming to do what no Liverpool player has done before or since: score hat-tricks in three consecutive matches. Balmer didn't disappoint the 51,435 fans who came to watch. After netting from the penalty spot, he added two more from open play to help clinch a 4–2 win over Arsenal. According to one newspaper report, the third was greeted with 'the loudest cheer Anfield has ever known'.

ROBBIE'S THREE IN FOUR

Robbie Fowler's first half hat-trick against Arsenal, in the space of just 4 minutes and 33 seconds, remains the fastest in Premiership history, and the quickest by any LFC player since the club was formed. It came at Anfield in August 1994, barely a year after the teenager had broken into the first team. Yet it was the fourth senior match in which he'd managed to hit the target three times. Only four other post-war Liverpool players have completed hat-tricks before the half-time whistle.

HAPPY AWAY DAYS FOR LUIS

Luis Suarez's hat-trick at Carrow Road in September 2012 made him the only Liverpool player to score three goals in the same away League fixture in successive seasons. Suarez, making his 50th Premier League appearance, gave what boss Brendan Rodgers described as a 'goalscoring masterclass' against Norwich City, helping his team to a 5–2 win. Just five months previously he'd grabbed all the goals in a 3–0 victory at the same venue. The last of them – a stunning lob from 45 yards out – completed his first-ever hat-trick for the Reds.

ABOVE: Beat that. Gordon Hodgson's hat-trick record is still intact, 77 years on

BELOW: Luis Suarez just can't get enough of playing against Norwich City at Carrow Road

DEBUT HAT-TRICKS

Ian St. John marked his first appearance in a Liverpool shirt with three goals against Everton. Unfortunately, it was in a Liverpool Senior Cup match so doesn't appear in the official records. St. John joined from Motherwell, for whom he'd once scored a hat-trick against Hibernian in the space of 150 seconds – one of the fastest ever recorded in Scottish football. Fellow Scot Bobby Graham, who made his first LFC appearance in a European Cup tie, is the only player to score three on his League debut. His hat-trick came in a 5–1 victory over Aston Villa in 1964, when he was only 19.

BELOW: Yossi Benayoun scores his second goal of the game against Havant & Waterlooville in 2008

FIRST HALF HAT-TRICKS
Michael Owen (v Newcastle, 30/8/98)
Robbie Fowler (v Arsenal, 28/8/94)
Ian Rush (v Luton Town, 29/10/83)
Phil Boersma (v Tottenham, 7/9/74)
John Evans (v Bristol Rovers, 15/9/54)

►► PENALTY HAT-TRICKS

Only one Liverpool player has scored three penalties in one match – and that was the spot-kick king himself, Jan Molby. He achieved the feat in a League Cup win against Coventry City in November 1986 – just three days before the teams met in a League game in which the big Dane scored from the spot yet again. A crowd of 19,179 were there to see Molby make history, including a six-year-old fan named Steven Gerrard, watching his first game at Anfield.

ABOVE: Picking his spot. Penalty king Jan Molby converted three in 90 minutes against Coventry City in the League Cup

THREE OFF THE BENCH

Irishman Steve Staunton was the first Liverpool player to score three after coming on as sub. He hit a second half hat-trick after replacing Ian Rush in a League Cup tie against Wigan Athletic on 4 October 1989. Skipper Steven Gerrard repeated the feat on 4 November 2010, in a 3–1 Europa League Group Stage victory over Napoli at Anfield.

◄◄ UNIQUE YOSSI

Israeli forward Yossi Benayoun is the only player to have scored hat-tricks for the same club in the Premier League, UEFA Champions League and FA Cup. Happily, that club is LFC, with Yossi's goals coming against Burnley, Besitkas and Havant & Waterlooville.

Transfers

Although the early transfer amounts paid by Liverpool remain a mystery, the first known fee is £75 for Preston North End forward Jimmy Ross in 1894. It was a wise investment, as, in 1895–96, he netted 23 times to help secure promotion to the top flight. By the summer of 2013, the club had broken their own transfer record 31 times.

▶▶ BIG ANDY'S HUGE FEE

Andy Carroll is Liverpool's record signing, agreeing terms with the club on the final, frantic day of the January 2011 transfer window. With just hours left before the deadline, Liverpool and Newcastle settled on a fee of £35 million for the England international, making him the most expensive British footballer ever.

At 22, Carroll was widely considered to be one of the game's hottest properties after helping his hometown club win promotion from the Championship in 2009–10, then hitting 11 goals in 10 Premier League matches. The 6ft 3in centre-forward scored twice on his Anfield debut, but then struggled to find the target on a regular basis. However, he came into his own in the second half of the 2010–11 season, heading the winner in the FA Cup semi-final victory over Everton at Wembley, then scoring in the final against Chelsea.

His form led to a place in England's 23-man squad for Euro 2012, but just weeks after that tournament ended, new club boss Brendan Rodgers agreed to loan him out to West Ham for the 2012–13 season.

RIGHT: The £35 million man. Andy Carroll checks in to his new home in January 2011

BELOW: Although signed by Gerard Houllier, former Auxerre striker Djibril Cisse played under Rafael Benitez

▶▶ RECORD BREAKERS

As well as the £35 million for Andy Carroll, Liverpool have splashed out the following club record fees down the years:

- **£100.** Paid to secure the signature of Preston and England forward Frank Becton in March 1895. Becton went on to score 42 goals in 86 games for the club.
- **£8,000.** George Patterson broke the bank to sign the giant centre-back Tom Bradshaw from Bury in 1930. Although Liverpool paid the same amount for both Sam English in 1933 and Matt Busby in 1936, they didn't exceed the figure for 16 years, making Bradshaw the club's longest-standing record buy.
- **£12,500.** In 1946, Liverpool and Everton took part in a bidding war for Newcastle striker Albert Stubbins. When both had agreed to meet his own board's valuation, Stubbins tossed a coin to decide which of the Merseyside clubs to meet first. He was so impressed with the Liverpool officials he cancelled the meeting with Everton and told them he was moving to Anfield.
- **£100,000.** Bill Shankly broke the six-figure barrier in 1968 to make Alun Evans the country's most expensive teenager. After seeing the 18-year-old Wolves forward run his defence ragged, Shankly was confident he'd have a bright future at Anfield. Sadly it wasn't to be, and Evans never quite fulfilled his potential. He left for Aston Villa four years later.
- **£440,000.** The sum paid to bring Kenny Dalglish from Celtic in 1977 set a new record for a transfer between British clubs. On his first game at Anfield Dalglish was greeted with a huge banner on the Kop declaring 'Kenny's Worth Every Penny'. How right that was.
- **£575,000.** Bob Paisley set a new benchmark when he signed livewire Craig Johnston from Middlesbrough. The attacking midfielder, who was born in South Africa but raised in Australia, was the first foreign player to hold the club's transfer record.

- **£1.9m.** Liverpool had never paid more than seven figures for a player, but when they did, it was with style. The sum spent on securing Peter Beardsley's services from Newcastle in 1987 was a million more than Kenny Dalglish splashed out on Watford's John Barnes just a month earlier. But the new No. 7 showed such devastating form he was quickly hailed as a bargain.
- **£11m.** Emile Heskey's capture from Leicester in March 2000 shattered the spending record set five years earlier when Stan Collymore arrived from Nottingham Forest for £8.5m. Heskey repaid the club's faith – and money – in the 2000–01 treble-winning season when he weighed in with 22 goals.
- **£14.5m.** Gerard Houllier's long pursuit of Djibril Cisse ended with him agreeing to move to Anfield for another record fee. But the striker never got to play for his fellow Frenchman. By the time he arrived from Auxerre, Houllier had departed and Rafa Benitez was in the manager's chair.
- **£20.5m.** The fee Rafa Benitez agreed to pay for Atletico Madrid hit-man Fernando Torres caused gasps – but not as many as the player himself in his first Anfield season. His phenomenal scoring record from his arrival in 2007 electrified the Premier League and made him an instant Anfield hero. But the love affair between player, club and fans was to come to an abrupt end after three and a half years.
- **£22.8m.** The signing of Luis Suarez from Ajax marked a new spending high for Liverpool – but the record lasted a matter of hours. The Uruguayan completed his move on 31 January 2011, becoming the most expensive player in Liverpool's history. But later that same day, boss Kenny Dalglish wrote a cheque for a much larger sum.

ABOVE RIGHT: In 1987 Peter Beardsley became the Reds' first seven-figure signing

RIGHT: Emile Heskey's signing broke a record lasting five years

FAREWELL FERNANDO

The sale of Fernando Torres to Chelsea shattered the transfer record between British clubs, boosting LFC coffers by an astonishing £50 million. Roman Abramovich made an initial £35 million bid to sign the Spanish striker five days before the January 2011 transfer window closed. Most Reds' supporters laughed it off, pointing to Torres' public statement at the start of the season: 'My commitment and loyalty to the club and to the fans is the same as it was on my first day when I signed.'

31 January turned into a day of high drama as Chelsea upped their offer to a level no one had expected. As the player re-iterated his desire to join them, Liverpool accepted the inevitable. Torres left the Melwood training ground for the last time, making his entrance at Stamford Bridge the following morning.

▶ WHEELER DEALERS

Rafa Benitez is the LFC manager most active in the transfer market, buying 60 players and selling 72 during his six years with the club. Benitez spent a record £231.2m on signings, and generated £161.7m in sales. The Spaniard had been at Anfield for just a month when he made his first move, capturing his fellow countryman, Josemi, from Malaga for £2m. In July 2010, the Serbian forward Milan Jovanovic, acquired from Standard Liege, became his last signing.

Although half of Liverpool's all-time most expensive players were bought by Benitez, he only broke the club spending record once, with the £20.2m purchase of Fernando Torres from Atletico Madrid. The post-war manager who broke it most often was Bill Shankly, who bought nine players for club record fees. They were Kevin Lewis (£13,000), Gordon Milne (£16,000), Ian St. John (£37,500), Peter Thompson (£40,000), Emlyn Hughes (£65,000), Tony Hateley (£96,000), Alun Evans (£100,000), John Toshack (£110,000) and Ray Kennedy (£180,000).

LFC'S RECORD SALES

Player	New club	Fee
Fernando Torres	Chelsea	£50m
Xabi Alonso	Real Madrid	£30m
Javier Mascherano	Barcelona	£17.25m
Robbie Keane	Tottenham	£16m
Robbie Fowler	Leeds United	£12.75m
Raul Meireles	Chelsea	£12m
Peter Crouch	Portsmouth	£11m
Michael Owen	Real Madrid	£8.5m
Momo Sissoko	Juventus	£8.2m
Craig Bellamy	West Ham	£7.5m

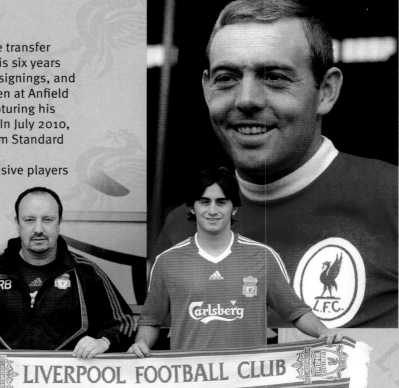

TOP: Ian St. John was a record £37,500 capture from Motherwell

ABOVE: Hello, Alberto. Aquilani was one of 60 players signed by Reds' boss Rafa Benitez

WHO BOUGHT WHO

Manager	First Signing	Last Signing	Record Signing
Bill Shankly	Sammy Reid	Ray Kennedy	Ray Kennedy (£180,000)
Bob Paisley	Peter McDonnell	Jim Beglin	Mark Lawrenson (£900,000)
Joe Fagan	Gary Gillespie	Wayne Harrison	Paul Walsh (£700,000)
Kenny Dalglish*	Steve McMahon	David Speedie	Ian Rush (£2.8m)
Graeme Souness	Mark Wright	Julian Dicks	Dean Saunders (£2.9m)
Roy Evans	Michael Stensgaard	Vergard Heggem	Stan Collymore (£8.5m)
Gerard Houllier	Jean Michel Ferri	Djibril Cisse	Djibril Cisse (£14.5m)
Rafael Benitez	Josemi Rey	Milan Jovanovic	Fernando Torres (£20.2m)
Roy Hodgson	Joe Cole	Paul Konchesky	Raul Meireles (£11.5m)
Kenny Dalglish**	Luis Suarez	Craig Bellamy	Andy Carroll (£35m)
Brendan Rodgers***	Fabio Borini	Phillipe Coutinho	Joe Allen (£15m)

* 1st spell   ** 2nd spell   ***Correct up to 1 June 2013

RIGHT: Heighway No. 9. The flying winger was a key member of the Reds' seventies side and an oustanding pick-up as a free transfer from amateur club Skelmersdale United

◀ THE BEST THINGS IN LIFE ARE FREE

Although never afraid to pay big money for the right man, Liverpool have landed some of their best players without having to part with a penny.

Steve Heighway was one. It was Bob Paisley's son who spotted the 22-year-old student playing for non-League Skelmersdale United in 1970, but Bill Shankly who signed him for free, then developed him into the dazzling winger who lit up Anfield throughout the 70s. Heighway's speed and skill prised open countless defences, and his crosses supplied the likes of Keegan, Toshack and Dalglish with endless goal chances. He was also on target 76 times himself in his 475 appearances. By the time he left the club in 1981, he'd helped the team win four League Championships, two European and UEFA Cups, and one FA Cup.

10 OTHER FANTASTIC FREE TRANSFERS

Player	Signed from	Year
Bob Paisley	Bishop Auckland	1939
Roger Hunt	Stockton Heath	1958
Ronnie Whelan	Home Farm	1979
Steve Staunton	Dundalk	1986
Gary McAllister	Coventry City	2000
Markus Babbel	Bayern Munich	2000
Jari Litmanen	Barcelona	2001
Fabio Aurelio	Valencia	2006
Maxi Rodriguez	Atletico Madrid	2010
Craig Bellamy	Manchester City	2011

RIGHT: Maxi for a minimum fee. Rogriguez arrived on a free transfer from Atletico Madrid

PERCENTAGE PROFITS

Although Liverpool made £29.5 million on the sale of Fernando Torres, it was by no means the biggest gain in percentage terms. Ray Clemence's move to Tottenham gave the club an incredible 1,567 per cent profit, compared to the 144 per cent on Torres. And that was after the keeper had helped them win five League Championships, three European Cups, two UEFA Cups and one FA and League Cup!

TITLE

Player	Bought for	Sold for	% Profit
Ray Clemence	£18,000	£300,000	1,567%
Kevin Keegan	£33,000	£500,000	1,415%
Ian Rush	£300,000	£3.2m	967%
Larry Lloyd	£50,000	£240,000	380%
Xabi Alonso	£10.7m	£30m	180%

Other Player Records

Success in football maybe the result of teamwork, but there'll always be room for outstanding individuals. Liverpool fans have seen more than their fair share: from feared strikers to extraordinary goalkeepers, from inspirational captains to substitutes who can turn a game with one flash of brilliance. This section celebrates those who've earned adoration from the crowd – and the highest plaudits from their fellow professionals.

THE MAN WITH THE GOLDEN BOOT

Ian Rush is the first British player to collect the Golden Boot – the prize given to the leading scorer in all of Europe's top League divisions. His achievement came at the end of 1983–84 when he hit 32 First Division goals and added 15 more in other competitions. It was another 20 years before a striker with an English club – Arsenal's Thierry Henry – received the honour.

▶ OUT ON HIS OWEN

In 2001, Michael Owen was named European Footballer of the Year – one of only six British players ever to win the award. He also became the first Liverpool man to get the honour, as Kevin Keegan, who won it in 1978 and 1979, had by then left Anfield for Hamburg.

It crowned a triumphant year for Owen, who had helped the team win a historic FA Cup, League Cup and UEFA Cup treble – as well as qualifying for the Champions League for the first time. Injuries may have restricted his appearances, but he still finished the campaign as the club's top scorer with 24 goals. The most memorable of all were undoubtedly his two in the last seven sensational minutes of the FA Cup final in Cardiff, when he overturned Arsenal's 1–0 lead.

ABOVE: So much, so young. A 22-year-old Michael Owen shows off the 2001 *Ballon D'Or*

Owen was 22 when he collected the Ballon D'Or, and his most effective scoring days were still ahead of him. For the next two successive seasons he would find the net 28 times. He left Liverpool for Real Madrid in 2004, having scored 158 times in 297 appearances.

◀ THE UNDISPUTED BEST

Terry McDermott was the first man in the English game to be named both Footballer of the Year and PFA Player of the Year in the same season. It was a fitting tribute to the lad from Kirkby who arrived from Newcastle in 1974, and initially struggled to hold down a first team place. But, by the time he won the awards in 1980, he had established himself as one of the most tireless and skilled midfielders in the country.

McDermott's scoring record was one that most strikers would be proud of – and many of those goals were spectacular. His header in the 7–0 rout of Tottenham in 1978 is still remembered as one of the finest ever seen at Anfield. A sublime chip against Everton a year earlier was named as 'Goal of the Season' by the BBC's *Match of the Day*. But perhaps his most important strike was at Rome's Stadio Olimpico in 1977, where he became the first Liverpool player to score in a European Cup final.

Capped 25 times by England; winner of four League Championship, three European Cup and two League Cup winner's medals – and part of arguably the best midfield in Liverpool's history – 'Terry Mac' remains one of Anfield's all-time greats.

LEFT: Terry McDermott was noted for sublime passing, endless running – and spectacular goals

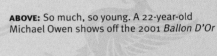
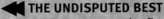

▶▶ DOING THE HONOURS

Three other Reds – Kenny Dalglish, Ian Rush and John Barnes – have all since won Footballer of the Year, and PFA Player of the Year accolades in the same season.

In 1995 and 1996 Robbie Fowler was named PFA Young Player of the Year in two successive seasons. Not surprising, as he finished those two campaigns with 31 and 36 goals respectively.

Steven Gerrard is one of only four men to have been voted Footballer of the Year, PFA Player of the Year and PFA Young Player of the Year during their careers. In addition, he won the PFA Fans' Player of the Year award in 2001 and 2009 – an honour also picked up by former team-mate Raul Meireles in 2011.

Football Writers' Footballer of the Year	PFA Player of the Year
1974 Ian Callaghan	1980 Terry McDermott
1976 Kevin Keegan	1983 Kenny Dalglish
1977 Emlyn Hughes	1984 Ian Rush
1979 Kenny Dalglish	1988 John Barnes
1980 Terry McDermott	2006 Steven Gerrard
1983 Kenny Dalglish	
1984 Ian Rush	**PFA Young Player of the Year**
1988 John Barnes	1983 Ian Rush
1989 Steve Nicol	1995 Robbie Fowler
1990 John Barnes	1996 Robbie Fowler
2009 Steven Gerrard	1998 Michael Owen
	2001 Steven Gerrard

ABOVE: John Barnes was the fourth Liverpool player to win both the FWA Footballer and PFA Player of the Year Awards in the same season in the 1980s

LEFT: Steve Nicol was the man who stopped John Barnes winning Footballer of the Year three times in a row

BEST TEAM IN THE LAND

The Professional Footballers' Association Team of the Year has been compiled by the players' union since the 1973–74 season. Steven Gerrard has been named in the team seven times – more than any other player during the Premier League era. Other LFC players to be picked in multiple seasons include Alan Hansen (6), Kenny Dalglish and Ian Rush (5), Mark Lawrenson and Graeme Souness (4) and John Barnes (3). In 1982–83, when Liverpool won a Championship and League Cup double, an unprecedented six of the 11 players selected for the PFA team were from LFC: Hansen, Lawrenson, Souness, Dalglish, Rush and Sammy Lee.

▼ BIG RON

At the end of the 2012–13 season, Steven Gerrard completed 10 years as club captain, equalling the record set by Alex Raisbeck who led the team on the pitch between 1899 and 1909. He also overtook the post-war record holder Ron Yeats, who skippered the side from 1961 to 1970.

Yeats, a former slaughterman from Dundee, was one of Bill Shankly's most important early signings, nicknamed 'The Colossus' by his manager because of his 6ft 2in frame and strapping physique. On the field, he led Liverpool to promotion from Division Two, then two subsequent League titles. He also became the first Reds player to be presented with the FA Cup, and just a year later led his team out in their first European final, against Borussia Dortmund at Hampden Park.

RIGHT: 'Captain Colossus' Ron Yeats with one of the two League Championships he won at Anfield

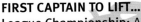

<table>
<tr><td colspan="2">FIRST CAPTAIN TO LIFT...</td></tr>
<tr><td>League Championship:</td><td>Alex Raisbeck</td></tr>
<tr><td>FA Cup:</td><td>Ron Yeats</td></tr>
<tr><td>League Cup:</td><td>Phil Thompson</td></tr>
<tr><td>UEFA Cup:</td><td>Tommy Smith</td></tr>
<tr><td>European Cup:</td><td>Emlyn Hughes</td></tr>
</table>

BORN TO LEAD

Andrew Hannah was the club's first captain, serving in the three seasons following LFC's formation. The Dumbartonshire-born defender was an excellent all-round sportsman who competed in the Highland Games. He was also no stranger to Anfield, having been part of Everton's 1890–91 Championship-winning team.

Fourteen Scots and 23 Englishmen have since held the captaincy. Ronnie Whelan is the only skipper from Ireland and Ian Rush the sole Welshman. John Barnes was the first to be born outside Britain and Ireland, while Finnish centre-back Sami Hyypia is the only club captain from mainland Europe.

► ALEXANDER THE GREAT

Alex Raisbeck was football's first superstar: skilful, handsome, and routinely described as the best defender of his generation. He was also a born leader, and the first Liverpool player to captain both his club and country.

The Scotsman made his name with Hibernian then moved to Anfield in 1898 for a club record fee of £350. He led the team to their first League Championship in 1901, and a second title five years later. 'Raisbeck dropped from the clouds', said one sports magazine. 'He employs pace and great judgement in tackling. In feeding his forwards he has few superiors.'

He stayed with the Reds for a decade, making 341 appearances. However, in 1901, when the Football Association imposed a maximum £4 a week limit on footballers' wages he was all set to leave. Only the club's offer of an additional job as 'bills inspector' – checking the public hoardings advertising forthcoming matches – persuaded him to remain. It's doubtful whether he did any actual inspecting, but it gave Liverpool a legitimate excuse to pay him more money.

OGDEN'S CIGARETTES.

A. G. RAISBECK.

RIGHT: Football's first 'superstar'. Liverpool skipper Alex Raisbeck was a Victorian-era pin-up

THREE LIONS...AND ONE LIVERBIRD

In 1921, Ephraim Longworth captained England in a 2–0 victory over Belgium in Brussels, becoming the first Liverpool skipper to lead the national side. The first post-war player to lead both club and country was Emlyn Hughes, who was handed the England armband for a match against Wales in May 1974 – and then kept it for six years.

LEADING FROM THE BACK

Only one goalkeeper has ever been appointed LFC captain at the start of the season. That was Derbyshire-born Harry Storer who took charge of on-the-field matters during the 1898–99 campaign.

PLAYING AND PRAYING

Former captain James Jackson was nicknamed 'The Parson' by fans, and with good reason: throughout his time at Anfield, he studied to be a Presbyterian minister. Jackson was in fact ordained shortly after his retirement from football in 1933, first practising as a church minister on the Isle of Man, then in Liverpool and Bournemouth.

ABOVE: The captain from Kirkby. Phil Thompson was skipper between 1979 and 1981

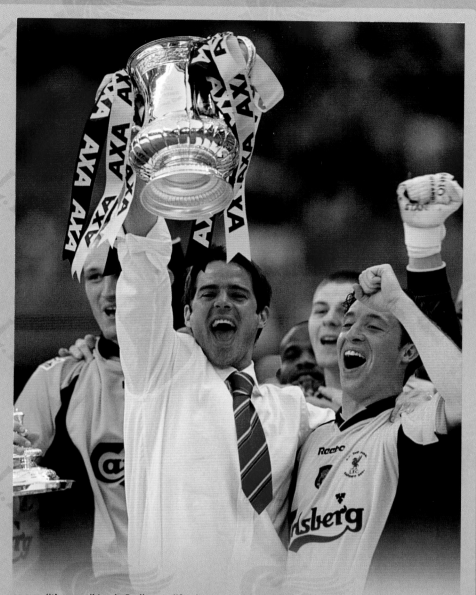

ABOVE: 'It's yours!' Jamie Redknapp lifts the 2001 FA Cup – at Robbie Fowler's insistence

▲ THIS ONE'S FOR YOU

Jamie Redknapp missed Liverpool's FA Cup final victory over Arsenal in 2001 – yet he still went onto the Millennium Stadium pitch to lift the trophy. Redknapp was club captain from 1999 to 2002, but was absent for every game during the Treble-winning campaign due to a serious knee injury. Sami Hyypia and Robbie Fowler – captain and vice-captain on the day of the dramatic late victory in Cardiff – both insisted he had the honour of holding the Cup aloft.

◄◄ SCOUSE SKIPPERS

Tom Bromilow was an original 'Scouser Tommy': one of the tens of thousands of young men from Liverpool who signed up to fight in World War I. When the hostilities ended he turned up at Anfield in Army uniform asking for a trial. A decade on, after making more than 300 appearances, he was appointed skipper.

Since then, Liverpool have had seven other captains who were born and raised on Merseyside.

Jack Balmer (Liverpool)
Laurie Hughes (Liverpool)
Johnny Wheeler (Crosby)
Ronnie Moran (Crosby)

Tommy Smith (Liverpool)
Phil Thompson (Kirkby)
Steven Gerrard (Huyton)

▶▶ THE MEN BETWEEN THE STICKS

Goalkeepers feature prominently in the list of players with most appearances for the club, with Ray Clemence (665), Bruce Grobbelaar (628) and Elisha Scott (468) all making the top 20.

Clemence was an ever-present in five different seasons during the 1970s and, after playing 336 back-to-back games, is second only to Phil Neal when it comes to consecutive first-team matches – and number of medals won. In a glittering Anfield career – in which he helped win five Championships, three European Cups, two UEFA Cups and an FA Cup – his exceptional season was 1978–79, when he kept a record 28 clean sheets, and conceded just 16 goals in 42 matches.

Bob Paisley rated Clemence as Liverpool's finest ever goalkeeper and he's generally considered to be one of the best that England has ever produced. However, he was restricted to 61 appearances in his international career due to the form of another brilliant contemporary, Peter Shilton.

ABOVE: Clean-sheet king Ray Clemence in action against Everton at Anfield

LIFE OF RILEY

Arthur Riley, who made his debut in 1925, was Liverpool's first-ever foreign signing. He'd been part of a South African national team that had toured England the year before, and beaten Liverpool in a friendly. He went on to make 338 appearances before his retirement in 1939.

▼ NO WAY PAST JOSE

Jose Manuel Reina began breaking records almost as soon as he arrived at Anfield. During his first season he kept clean sheets in 11 successive matches – more than any other LFC keeper. In the final game of the campaign, he saved three of West Ham's four penalties in the FA Cup final shoot-out in Cardiff.

That same year, 'Pepe' collected the first of three successive 'Golden Gloves' awards – the prize given to the Premier League keeper with most shut-outs during a season. Along the way he set a new Liverpool record by reaching 50 clean sheets in 92 matches – compared to Ray Clemence's 95. He also took just 197 games reach 100 clean sheets,

breaking another of Clemence's long-standing records.

In December 2012 Reina was between the posts for a 3–0 victory at Queens Park Rangers – a Premier League match in which he overtook Elisha Scott's 127 League shut-outs. By the end of the 2012–13 season he'd recorded 177 clean sheets in total – still a way behind Clemence (323) and Bruce Grobbelaar (267), both of whom made many more appearances.

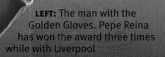

LEFT: The man with the Golden Gloves. Pepe Reina has won the award three times while with Liverpool

CLEAN SHEET KINGS

Goalkeeper	Matches	Clean Sheets
Ray Clemence	665	323
Bruce Grobbelaar	628	267
Jose Reina	394	177
Elisha Scott	468	137
Tommy Lawrence	390	133

▶▶ ONE DAY, TWO KEEPERS

Sander Westerveld was a hero during the 2000–01 treble-winning season, playing in every one of the club's 57 matches. But, when his form dipped at the start of the following campaign, boss Gerard Houllier took drastic action – buying two replacements in one day.

Hours after breaking the transfer record for a British goalkeeper, by paying £6 million for Coventry City's Chris Kirkland, he splashed out £4.8 million to recruit Polish international Jerzy Dudek from Feyenoord. Westerveld was gone within a month.

RUSSELL'S RECORD

Russell Crossley played most of his games during the Reds' early 1950s downturn, so it comes as no surprise that he has the worst average of any goalkeeper in the club's history. The Yorkshireman conceded 138 goals in 73 games – an average of 1.89 per match. He made his last 19 appearances in the 1953–54 relegation season.

DOING THE DUDEK

In a poll conducted by UEFA, Jerzy Dudek's famous double-save from Andriy Shevchenko in the 2005 Champions League final was voted the "Greatest Champions League Moment of All-Time". There were just three minutes of extra time remaining when he blocked the AC Milan striker's powerful header, then incredibly diverted his follow-up shot over the top from just a yard out. The poll put Dudek's heroics above Zinedine Zidane's volleyed goal in the 2002 final, and Manchester United's last-gasp winner in 1999.

UNDERSTUDIES

Scott Carson and Chris Kirkland may have gone on to win England caps but they had to largely settle for being understudies while at Anfield. The club's tradition of having world-class Number Ones has meant several other excellent keepers being restricted to extended spells in the reserves and on the bench.

One of the longest-serving understudies was Steve Ogrizovic who signed from Chesterfield in 1977, then spent five seasons in the shadow of the great Ray Clemence. He later played for Coventry for 16 years, breaking their all-time appearance record with 601 games. By the time he retired in 2000, he'd become one of only four players to play top-flight football in four different decades.

ABOVE: Flying Dutchman, Sander Westerveld played in 57 games during the treble-winning season

BELOW: Jerzy's finest hour. Dudek's heroics helped Liverpool to win the UEFA Champions League final shoot-out in Istanbul

STRONG MAN

Geoff Strong was Liverpool's first substitute, coming on to replace the injured Chris Lawler in a 1–1 home League draw with West Ham on 15 September 1965. He was also the first sub to score – hitting a second-half equaliser in the same match.

Seven months later, he was in the side that lined up against Celtic in the second leg semi-final of the European Cup Winners' Cup, a tournament in which subs still weren't permitted. That turned out to be fortunate for Liverpool, as Strong had to stay on the Anfield pitch despite sustaining a serious knee injury before the interval. Midway through the second half he defied excruciating pain to rise above the Celtic defence and head home Ian Callaghan's cross. It was the goal that secured the team's first appearance in a European final.

SUBSTITUTE RULES...SEASON BY SEASON

1965–66: Substitutes first permitted. One per team, and only to be used to replace an injured player.

1967–68: Substitutions permitted for tactical reasons. Two subs allowed in European ties.

1968–69: Three subs allowed in European ties.

1969–70: Five subs allowed in European ties.

1986–87: Two subs permitted in domestic Cup games.

1987–88: Two subs permitted in League matches.

1994–95: Five subs permitted in League matches.

1997–98: Seven subs allowed in European ties.

1998–99: Five subs allowed in domestic Cup games.

ABOVE: Geoff Strong played 201 times for Liverpool but is more famous for being the first-ever substitute and first substitute to score for the Reds

RIGHT: More than half of Ryan Babel's 146 appearances were as a substitute

◀ LATE, AS USUAL

More than half of Ryan Babel's 146 matches were as a substitute. The Dutchman made his debut as a sub in a 2–1 win at Aston Villa, and then came off the bench a further 80 times during his three years at Anfield.

As well as making 62 appearances as a No. 12, David Fairclough was also an unused substitute in 74 matches. Among his many goalscoring records as a sub, he was the first one to score in FA Cup, League Cup and European Cup matches.

MOST APPEARANCES OFF THE BENCH

Ryan Babel	81
Vladimir Smicer	74
Danny Murphy	71
David Fairclough	62
Patrik Berger	60
Robbie Fowler	60

▶▶ GAYLE FORCE

In April 1981, Howard Gayle became the first Liverpool substitute to be subbed. But his 61 minutes on the pitch against Bayern Munich inspired the team to one of their most memorable European Cup performances.

The Germans had held the Reds to a 0–0 draw at Anfield and were confident of victory on home soil. But their well-prepared plans were thrown into chaos when Kenny Dalglish limped off after just nine minutes, to be replaced by a youngster whose speed, power and direct approach took them completely unawares. The Bayern defenders resorted to fouling the Liverpool-born winger repeatedly, finally provoking him into retaliation which led to a booking. Concerned that Gayle would get into further trouble, Bob Paisley withdrew him after 70 minutes. But his team went on to earn a 1–1 draw, and a victory on away goals.

Despite his stunning cameo, Gayle made just five appearances for the Reds. He'll be remembered not only as the club's first black player, but as the man who helped secure a place in a second successive European Cup final.

ABOVE: Game-changer. Howard Gayle's cameo appearance caused mayhem in Munich

LEFT: Unsung Hero. Half-time substitute Didi Hamann did as much as anyone to over-turn AC Milan's lead in the 2005 UEFA Champions League final.

◀◀ IMPACT SUBS: FOUR MORE WHO CHANGED THE GAME

- David Fairclough v Everton, League, 4 March 1976
  A year before his famous St. Etienne appearance, teenage sub Fairclough stunned Anfield with a mesmerising 88th minute run from the halfway line, ending with a perfectly struck shot into the Anfield Road net. The 1–0 win sent the Reds to the top of the table.
- Ian Rush v Everton, FA Cup, 20 May 1989
  Everton had snatched a last gasp equaliser in normal time. But Rush, who had replaced John Aldridge after 72 minutes, used his fresh legs to maximum effect, getting on the scoresheet twice in extra time to win the Cup for Liverpool. Amazingly, Everton's two goals were from Stuart McCall, who had also come on as a sub.
- Dietmar Hamann v AC Milan, Champions League, 25 May 2005
  Dudek and Gerrard got the headlines but it was the dominant German, coming on for the second half, who neutralised AC Milan's midfield threat and allowed his team-mates to push forward, clawing back a 3–0 deficit. Hamann was also on target in the penalty shoot-out.
- Djibril Cisse v CSKA Moscow, Super Cup, 26 August 2005
  With 11 minutes of the Super Cup final left, Liverpool were trailing 1–0. Enter the big Frenchman, who levelled within three minutes, then added a third in extra time as the team won 3–1.

TWICE ON THE BENCH

Michael Thomas, a substitute in the Reds' 1995 League Cup final against Bolton, had also been an Arsenal substitute in the 1987 final – when they lined up against Liverpool.

MOST RED CARDS

With six red cards in his career, Steven Gerrard has been sent off more times than any Liverpool player. However, his average number of dismissals per game is far outweighed by both Igor Biscan and Javier Mascherano.

The former Argentinian midfielder also has an unenviable record for yellow cards. He was cautioned 10 times in the 2009–10 season, equalling the club record set in 2003–04 by El-Hadji Diouf.

RIGHT: Not again! Gerrard picks up the sixth red card of his career at Old Trafford in January 2011

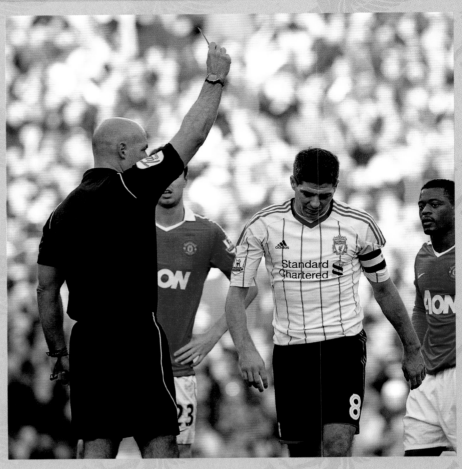

RED CARD TABLE

Steven Gerrard	6
Igor Biscan	3
Jamie Carragher	3
Javier Mascherano	3
Ian St. John	3

• Dietmar Hamann also received three red cards, although one was later rescinded

FAIR PLAY TO THEM

As well as being two of the club's longest servants, both Billy Liddell and Ian Callaghan had incredible disciplinary records. Neither was ever sent off and, in 534 games, Liddell never picked up a single caution. Callaghan almost made it through his record-breaking run of 857 appearances without a blemish. But he was booked in the 1978 League Cup final replay against Nottingham Forest – his 856th match.

EMERGENCY KEEPERS

When Jose Enrique put on the gloves in a Premier League fixture at Newcastle in 2012, he became the third Liverpool outfield player to replace a dismissed goalkeeper. Enrique went between the sticks following Pepe Reina's red card in the 83rd minute, as Brendan Rodgers had already used the maximum three substitutes.

It was the first time it had happened since the Anfield Premiership derby in 1999, when Sander Westerveld was sent off, and Steve Staunton had to deputise for the last 16 minutes. The Reds lost both of those games, but neither emergency keeper conceded.

However, it was a different story in the 1992 European Cup Winners' Cup clash at Spartak Moscow. On 84 minutes, with the match level at 2–2, Bruce Grobbelaar was given his marching orders for bringing down an opposition striker in the penalty area. Full-back David Burrows was beaten by the resulting spot kick, and another Spartak strike a minute from time, leaving the Reds as 4–2 losers.

LEFT: All yours. Reina hands his shirt and gloves to Jose Enrique following his dismissal at St James' Park

The 1974 Charity Shield match was a bad tempered affair, culminating in the dismissals of Kevin Keegan and Leeds' captain Billy Bremner – the first British players to be sent off at Wembley. The two were ordered off the field after a 60th minute brawl. They then outraged the FA authorities by throwing their shirts to the ground in disgust as they walked to the tunnel. Both players received heavy fines, and were banned for 11 matches.

LEFT: 'No arguments'. Billy Bremner and Kevin Keegan were the first British players to be sent off at Wembley

A CAUTIONARY TALE

In 2012–13 Luis Suarez became the first Liverpool player to receive ten Premier League yellow cards in one season. The Uruguayan played in 33 of the first 34 league matches before he was suspended after the Chelsea match in April (during which he also picked up his tenth yellow card). On the plus side, however, Suarez did score 23 Premier League goals during the campaign.

AND THEN THERE WERE NINE...

The first recorded instance of two Liverpool players being sent off in a match was in 1925 when centre-back Jock McNab was dismissed for kicking a Newcastle player at Anfield. Shortly afterwards, his team-mate Walter Wadsworth followed him down the tunnel for punching an opponent who had allegedly thrown mud at him. The tough and hot-tempered Wadsworth, who once hit a Sheffield United fan who had been abusing him from the terraces, was banned for the rest of the season.

There have been three other double sending offs since then – most recently in the 4–0 defeat at Tottenham in 2011, when both Charlie Adam and Martin Skrtel saw red.

NAUGHTY DEVILS

The Premier League clash between Liverpool and Manchester United has become noted for red cards, with 14 issued between 1992 and 2012. United captain Nemanja Vidic has been dismissed three times – more than any player in one top-flight fixture. Liverpool players saw red eight times in League and cup matches between the two teams during the same period. But things were very different before the Premier League era. In fact Liverpool went 97 years, and 137 competitive games, against United before having a player sent off. That was Gary Ablett in October 1991.

BELOW: Repeat offender. United defender Nemanja Vidic has been dismissed three times while playing against Liverpool

NIGHTMARE START

Joe Cole is the only Liverpool player to be sent off on his League debut. The new signing from Chelsea received a straight red for a two-footed challenge on Arsenal's Laurent Koscielny on the opening day of the 2010–11 Premier League season at Anfield.

FIVE FAST REDS
Sami Hyypia 3 mins
(v Manchester United, 5 April 2003)
Steven Gerrard 18 mins
(v Everton, 25 March 2006)
Alexander Doni 25 mins
(v Blackburn Rovers, 10 April 2012)
Charlie Adam 28 mins
(v Tottenham, 18 September 2011)
Ryan Babel 30 mins
(v Benfica, 1 April 2010)

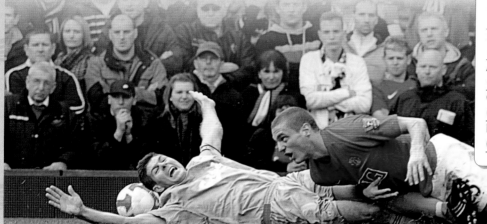

Internationals

Liverpool's first international player was local-born Harry Bradshaw who appeared in England's 6–0 victory over Ireland on 20 February 1897. The latest to be capped is Raheem Sterling, who made his England debut against Sweden on 14 November 2012.

Between those years, there have been internationals representing 44 nations on the LFC books. The club has supplied those countries with captains and leading goalscorers. Liverpool players have appeared at every World Cup since 1950. Some have even returned with winner's medals.

The number of Reds chosen to represent their countries is a reflection of the club's own success. England has been particularly dependent on the supply line from Anfield. In 1980 the home nation called up six Reds players to the squad for the European Championships in Italy– the biggest-ever contingent from a single club.

Anfield itself has staged international matches and is the only Premier League stadium to host 'home' fixtures by two different countries. As well as England, who've used the ground eight times since 1889, it's also been a 'home' venue for Wales on three occasions. The Welsh FA first chose it for their World Cup qualifier against Scotland in 1977. A crowd of 50,850 saw the 'away' side win 2–0, with Kenny Dalglish heading home the second.

TOP LEFT: Scouse Lion. Steven Gerrard is the first Liverpool player to make more than 100 England appearances

BOTTOM LEFT: A legend for for his country as well as his clubs, Kenny Dalglish won a record number of Scottish caps

BELOW: 'The Kaiser'. Reds midfielder Didi Hamann playing one of his 59 matches for Germany

BELOW RIGHT: Fernando Torres's World Cup success with Spain came while he was at Liverpool

England

▶▶ CAP THAT

With 102 international appearances, Steven Gerrard is Liverpool's most capped England player ever. He made his debut against Ukraine in May 2000, and first captained the side in a friendly against Sweden four years later. Gerrard has served under five England managers and played in three European Championships and two World Cups. By the summer of 2013 he stood at No. 6 in the all-time England appearances list. In February 2013 he was voted England Player of the Year for the second time, having first collected the award in 2007.

ENGLAND CAPS WHILE AT LFC*

Steven Gerrard	102	
Michael Owen	60	(77)
Emlyn Hughes	59	(63)
Ray Clemence	56	(61)
Phil Neal	50	
John Barnes	48	(79)
Phil Thompson	42	
Jamie Carragher	38	
Emile Heskey	35	(62)
Roger Hunt	34	
Peter Beardsley	34	(59)

*Total caps, including while with other clubs, in brackets

CAPTAIN FANTASTIC

Steven Gerrard is the 11th Liverpool player to lead England out, and, with 27 appearances as skipper, he's worn the armband more than any other. Ephraim Longworth was the first, captaining the team in a friendly against Belgium in May 1921. He was also Liverpool's oldest, at 33 years, 232 days. Michael Owen is the youngest, assuming responsibility at 22 years, 125 days, as England beat Paraguay 4–0 at Anfield in April 2002.

ENGLAND CAPTAIN APPEARANCES WHILE AT LFC*

Steven Gerrard	26	
Emlyn Hughes	23	
Kevin Keegan	7	(31)
Phil Thompson	6	
Michael Owen	6	(8)
Paul Ince	3	(7)
Peter Beardsley	1	
Ray Clemence	1	
Phil Neal	1	
Ephraim Longworth	1	
Tom Lucas	1	

*Total captain's appearances, including while with other clubs, in brackets

LEFT: More than a quarter of Steven Gerrard's 102 England appearances have been as captain

BELOW LEFT: 'It was definitely over the line!' Hunt gets a close-up view of Geoff Hurst's controversial goal at the 1966 World Cup final

◀◀ HUNT FOR GOALS

The Liverpool player with most goals in one England match is Roger Hunt, who hit four in the 10–0 demolition of the United States. That game in New York in 1964 came just five months after he bagged four in Liverpool's 6–1 League victory over Stoke at Anfield. Hunt kept up a superb strike record for his country, scoring 18 goals in 34 appearances. In 1966 he was in the team that beat Germany 4–2, becoming the first Liverpool player to collect a World Cup winner's medal.

HAT-TRICK IN MUNICH

England's record 5–1 away win over Germany in September 2001 came entirely from goals by Liverpool players. Michael Owen got a hat-trick in the World Cup qualifier in Munich, with Steven Gerrard and Emile Heskey adding the others. As of May 2013, Owen is the fourth highest England scorer of all time, with 26 of his 40 goals coming during his Anfield days.

LEFT: Hat-trick hero. Michael Owen celebrates his third goal in the 5–1 victory over Germany in Munich

SHORT AND SWEET

Reds defender Martin Kelly has the shortest England career on record. His only appearance so far was as an 88th minute substitute against Norway in May 2012. Although he only played two minutes officially, the referee's added time meant his actual spell on the pitch was 6 minutes, 53 seconds.

EVERYTHING COMES TO HE WHO WAITS

The longest-ever wait between England appearances is 11 years and 49 days – the gap between Ian Callaghan's showing in the 2–0 victory over France in 1966, and his return to international action in a 0–0 draw with Switzerland in September 1977. The Reds' winger played in two games at the 1966 World Cup, but was left out for the final. It took another 43 years before FIFA ruled that all England's squad members should be presented with winner's medals. Cally – along with former Liverpool team-mate Gerry Byrne – collected his in June 2009.

PASS IT ON...

The captaincy passed between a record four players during England's 3–1 friendly victory over Serbia and Montenegro on 3 June 2003 – and three of those were Liverpool men. Michael Owen led the team out but a series of substitutions meant his team-mates Jamie Carragher and Emile Heskey went on to wear the armband, along with Manchester United's Gary Neville. According to the official records, only Owen is listed as captain. The others are classed as 'temporary custodians'.

FOR AND AGAINST

Two Liverpool players have represented other countries as well as England. Gordon Hodgson played for his native South Africa as an amateur before winning the first of his three England caps in 1930. Tommy Smith, who won his sole cap in 1971, went on to play for Team America in the 1976 Bicentennial Tournament – against England.

RIGHT: Nice while it lasted. Reds defender Martin Kelly made the briefest-ever England appearance against Norway

GYPSY KING

Victorian star Raby Howell was the first gypsy to play for Liverpool and England. The diminutive midfielder, who was born in a Romany caravan in Yorkshire, won his first cap while with his previous club, Sheffield United. He signed for the Reds in 1898 and made his second and last appearance for the national side a year later.

Other Home Nations

SCOTLAND CAPS WHILE AT LFC*	
Kenny Dalglish	55 (102)
Graeme Souness	37 (54)
Billy Liddell	29
Steve Nicol	27
Alan Hansen	26

*Total caps, including while with other clubs, in brackets

◀◀ TARTAN TITAN

Kenny Dalglish is the most capped player in Scotland's history, making 102 appearances for his country during a 15-year international career. With 30 goals, he's also the joint top scorer along with Denis Law. Kenny made his debut as a substitute in a 1971 European Championship qualifier against Belgium. He played at the World Cup in Germany three years later, then the 1978 and 1982 tournaments in Argentina and Spain. He won 55 of his caps while at Anfield, and played his last five Scotland games during his first spell as Liverpool boss.

Liverpool's second most capped Scot is Graeme Souness, who made 37 of his appearances while at Liverpool. Billy Liddell, Steve Nicol and Alan Hansen won all their caps as Liverpool players

LIDDELL BRITAIN

As well as his 29 Scotland appearances, Billy Liddell played twice for a Great Britain side made up of internationals from the four home nations. The first game – dubbed The Match of The Century – was against a Rest of Europe XI in 1947. A crowd of 135,000 were at Glasgow's Hampden Park to see the British team win 6–1. Eight years later the two sides met again at Windsor Park, Belfast, in a match to celebrate the 75th anniversary of the Irish FA. Liddell was one of only two players from the original British side to be selected for the second fixture. England's legendary winger, Sir Stanley Matthews, was the other.

▼ ENTER THE DRAGON

Ian Rush is Wales' all-time leading scorer with 28 goals in 73 games. His first was in a 3–0 win over Northern Ireland in 1982, and the last in a 2–1 victory over Estonia in 1994. All but two of his international goals came during his spells with Liverpool. With 73 caps, Rush ranks fourth in his country's all-time appearance list, just ahead of former Reds' full-back Joey Jones who won 72 caps.

LEFT: Kenny Dalglish is Scotland's all-time joint-top scorer with 30 goals

BELOW: Wearing red for his country as well as his club, Ian Rush made 73 appearances for Wales

DUAL INTERNATIONALS

Before partition in 1922, the team selected by the Belfast-based Irish Football Association (IFA) represented both north and south. The IFA continued to call its team 'Ireland' despite the formation of a rival national side by the Dublin-based Football Association of Ireland (FAI). Until 1950, there were actually two rival 'Irelands' selected by both organisations, and around 40 so-called 'dual internationals' turned out for both teams. One of the earliest was Liverpool winger Bill Lacey who made 23 appearances for the IFA, then another three for the FAI. The last of those came in 1930 when he was 41 – making him the Republic of Ireland's oldest ever player.

◀◀ TWO-TIME TOSH
In 1994, John Toshack became the first ex-Liverpool player to manage his national side. Incredibly his spell in charge of Wales lasted just one game, due to his resignation following a 3–1 defeat by Norway. Toshack, who had been capped 40 times as a player, was reappointed to the job in 2004. Six years later he stepped down a second time after his team were beaten by Montenegro in a Euro 2012 qualifier.

LEFT: John Toshack, with his assistant Dean Saunders, during his second spell as Wales's national coach

ELISHA'S NO. 1
Despite Liverpool's close association with Northern Ireland, the club has had no active internationals from the country for more than three quarters of a century. The last was goalkeeper Elisha Scott, who made his debut against Scotland in 1920 and went on to make 31 appearances over the next 16 years.

ON THE MARK
The Republic of Ireland's record victory – an 8–0 thrashing of Malta in a 1984 European Championship qualifier – was partly thanks to two goals from Mark Lawrenson. Liverpool's Preston-born defender had made his international debut as a teenager seven years earlier, being eligible for a cap because his mother was Irish.

STEVE'S TREBLE
Throughout their history the Republic of Ireland have only qualified for three World Cup finals: in 1990, 1994 and 2002. Former Reds' full-back Steve Staunton is the only player to have appeared in all of them. As well as being the first Irish player to win a century of caps, Staunton also managed the national side between January 2006 and October 2007.

▶▶ IRISH BLOOD
Reds' striker Ray Houghton scored the Republic of Ireland's first ever goal in a major tournament, heading the winner against England at the 1988 European Championships. The Glaswegian was among many players who qualified for the Irish team through ancestry, and who were given their debuts by Jack Charlton. Others included Scouser John Aldridge, Birkenhead-born Jason McAteer and Londoner Phil Babb.

RIGHT: A Scotsman and an Irishman. Glaswegian Ray Houghton represented the Republic at two World Cup finals

Rest of the World

ABOVE: Finland's main man. Jari Litmanen is his country's most-capped player and record goalscorer

LEAGUE OF NATIONS

Liverpool have had 219 internationals who won their caps during, before or after their time with the club. Those players have appeared for 44 different countries – 87 of them for England. The nations most represented are:

1.	England	87
2.	Scotland	44
3.	Wales	23
4.	Republic of Ireland	17
5.	Northern Ireland	8
6.	France	7
=	Spain	7
7.	Norway	6
=	Holland	6
8.	Argentina	4
=	Denmark	4
=	Germany	4

THE JARI YEARS

Of all Liverpool's internationals, Jari Litmanen and Rigobert Song have the most caps – both playing 137 times for Finland and Cameroon respectively. Litmanen's Finland career stretched from 1989 to 2010, making him the only footballer to play internationals in four different decades. One of those games was at Anfield in 2001, when his side lost to England in a World Cup qualifier. A year earlier, he hit the opening goal in a 2–1 victory over Wales, becoming the first player to score at the Millennium Stadium. Litmanen was succeeded as national captain by Finland's second most capped player, Sami Hyypia, who made 71 of his 105 international appearances while at Liverpool.

OUT OF AFRICA

Liverpool's first players from outside the UK and Ireland were both South Africans. Goalkeeper Arthur Riley and striker Gordon Hodgson were part of an amateur Springbok side that played a series of friendlies in Britain in 1924. On 1 October that year the tourists beat Liverpool 5–2 at Anfield, with Hodgson getting a hat-trick. The Liverpool board offered him and Riley professional contracts soon afterwards No transfer fees were involved, and each player agreed to cross continents for just £90 travelling and hotel expenses.

SUAREZ SUCCESS

In November 2011, Luis Suarez became the first Liverpool player to score four goals in an international match since Roger Hunt 47 years previously. The Uruguayan's strikes came on home soil in a 4–0 World Cup qualifier against Chile. Earlier that year Suarez inspired his country to their 15th Copa America success, scoring four times during the competition, including the opener in the final. He was later voted Player of the Tournament.

RIGHT: Four goal hero. Luis Suarez in free scoring mood against Chile

▲ DIDI'S THE MAN

Dietmar Hamann was the last player to score at the old Wembley, striking Germany's winning goal against England in October 2000, shortly before the stadium was demolished. Two years later he became the first serving Liverpool player to take part in a World Cup final since 1966. Hamann's fellow countryman Karl-Heinz Riedle played in the 1990 final, seven years before his move to Anfield.

ABOVE: 'Goodbye Wembley'. Hamann's right-footed rocket was the last goal scored at the old stadium

BELOW: Javier Mascherano was a Liverpool player when he was appointed captain of Argentina in 2010

REIGNING IN SPAIN

In 2010 Fernando Torres became the second Liverpool player to be part of a World Cup winning side, coming on as an extra-time substitute in Spain's 1–0 victory over Holland. His team-mates included ex-Reds Xabi Alonso, along with Jose Reina and Alvaro Arbeloa, who both made the subs' bench. Among his opponents was Liverpool's Dirk Kuyt – one of only three Dutch players in the starting XI not to be cautioned during the final.

STIG OF THE CUP

Stig Inge Bjornebye was Liverpool's sole representative at the 1994 World Cup, making three appearances for Norway in the United States. The club has had six Norwegian internationals on its books, including John Arne Riise, who has won a record 110 caps.

VLADIMIR – OUR CZECH MATE

Reds fans will always remember Vladimir Smicer for his exploits in the 2005 Champions League final, when he scored both from open play and in the penalty shoot-out. But he's a hero back in his home country, too. The Czech is one of only seven players to score at three European Championships, hitting the target in 1996, 2000 and 2004. He's now the general manager of the Czech national team.

▶▶ GOLDEN BOY

While at Liverpool, midfielder Javier Mascherano became only the second Argentinian in history to win two Olympic gold medals. He picked up his first at the 2004 Games in Greece, and his second four years later in Beijing as one of his country's over-23 players. Mascherano went on to captain the national team at the 2010 World Cup.

LONG SONG

Ex-Reds full-back Rigobert Song is the only African to have played at four World Cup finals. He also has the unhappy distinction of being the only player to be sent off at two consecutive tournaments. Song made his international debut for Cameroon at just 17, and subsequently featured in the 1994, 1998, 2002 and 2010 finals. He retired from international duty soon afterwards as Cameroon's most-capped player of all-time.

Other Records

Liverpool have packed out stadiums around Britain and Europe, recorded some of English football's highest season-average attendances, and attracted worldwide television audiences numbered in the hundreds of millions. Not bad for a club that played its first competitive home game in front of just 200 people!

From their first seasons in the Football League, the Reds have been a magnet for spectators, appealing first to their large local support, and then gradually drawing in followers from outside the city. Today they boast a massive global fan-base, with huge numbers of supporters stretching from Ireland to America; from Scandinavia to the Far East. They play to full houses on pre-season tours, packing out stadiums in countries as far away as Singapore, Thailand and Malaysia.

There are many reasons for the club's continuing ability to catch the imagination of supporters around the globe. From its legendary players and inspirational managers, to its incredible record of honours, to its unique relationship with the fans who stand on the Anfield terraces. Then there's a 121-year timeline full of stirring tales of fight-backs and triumphs against the odds. It might be possible to buy future success in football. But history is priceless.

FAR RIGHT: Fans showed their devotion at a training session in Kuala Lumpur, Malaysia

RIGHT: When the Reds sold out Tianhe stadium when Guangdong Sunray Cave provided the opposition in 2011

BELOW: (left to right) Lucas Leiva, Jamie Carragher, Steven Gerrard and Luis Suarez walk off the Anfield pitch at half-time in the match against Zenit St Petersburg in the 2012–13 UEFA Europa League. The Reds won 3–1 on the night but lost on away goals

BOTTOM RIGHT: Fans can't get enough Liverpool FC merchandise at Japan's Narita Airport

Attendances

In the 2012–13 season Liverpool attracted the club's highest crowds of the Premier League era – with an average of 44,748 passing through the turnstiles for every home League game. A figure like that is impressive enough, but it's still far short of some of the attendances Anfield has witnessed in the past.

WOLVES PACK THEM IN

Liverpool's highest home attendance came on 2 February 1952, when 61,905 fans watched an FA Cup fourth round tie against Wolves. The match became famous for the record gate, and for Liverpool boss Don Welsh outmanoeuvring post-war football's most celebrated tactician. Few expected the struggling manager to get the better of opposite number, Stan Cullis, who was then busily turning his side into the most feared team in the country. But, seconds before the kick-off, Welsh ordered left-winger Billy Liddell to switch positions with centre-forward Cyril Done, throwing Wolves' plans to stifle the Scotsman into chaos. By the time they re-organised their defence, Liverpool were ahead, thanks to goals from Done and Bob Paisley. They eventually ran out 2–1 winners, only to be knocked out in the next round of the Cup by Burnley.

This was only the third time an Anfield attendance went through the 60,000 barrier. It broke the previous record set 18 years earlier when Tranmere Rovers drew Liverpool at home at the same stage of the competition. Rather than host the game at Prenton Park, the Birkenhead club elected to play the tie on the other side of the Mersey.

CAPITAL CROWD

Multiple clashes between Liverpool and Chelsea have become common in the modern era, with the clubs facing each other in the Premier League and domestic and European cup competitions. Still, the teams at least get a break between games. Unlike in 1949, when they met twice – in just 24 hours.

On Boxing Day, the Reds travelled to the capital where a 1–1 draw at Stamford Bridge kept them on top of Division One. The following afternoon a 58,757 crowd watched the teams draw two goals apiece. It was the biggest-ever League gate at Anfield and came during the height of the post-war boom when attendances around the country were at their peak. Four of Liverpool's five highest home League crowds came in the 1940s. The other match was at the end of the 1972–73 season when Liverpool paraded the Championship trophy.

BELOW: Packed to the rafters. The old 'standing' Kop could house more than 20,000 spectators

▼ ANFIELD'S SUPERSIZED GATES: FIVE HIGHEST (CUP COMPETITIONS)

Opposition	Date	Competition	Attendance
Wolves	2/2/1952	FA Cup, Round 4	61,905
Tranmere Rovers	27/1/1934	FA Cup, Round 4	61,036
Notts County	29/1/1949	FA Cup, Round 4	61,003
Burnley	20/2/1963	FA Cup, Round 4 (R)	57,906
Chelsea	27/2/1932	FA Cup, Round 6	57,804

ANFIELD'S SUPERSIZED GATES: FIVE HIGHEST (LEAGUE)

Opposition	Date	Attendance
Chelsea	27/12/1949	58,757
Middlesbrough	23/10/1948	57,561
Bolton	11/9/1948	56,561
Leicester	28/4/1973	56,202
Burnley	6/9/1947	56,074

THE BOY FROM BARCA

Traffic wardens around Anfield were reputed to have done record business on 14 April 1976. The reason? Liverpool were on the verge of a second European final. And Johann Cruyff – then the biggest star in world football – was in town.

The three-times European Player of the Year had once helped Ajax demolish the Reds 5–1 in a European Cup tie in Amsterdam. But in this UEFA Cup semi, Cruyff and his Barcelona team-mates were up against a more ruthless and disciplined force. The first leg at the Camp Nou brought one of Liverpool's most famous European performances to date, with John Toshack's goal earning a 1–0 win. In the second leg Anfield was at its loudest and most pulsating as 55,104 fans crammed in to witness a 1–1 draw, and a 2–1 aggregate victory.

Almost a year after this triumph, another 55,000-plus home crowd witnessed an even more memorable night, as Liverpool staged a dramatic comeback to beat St. Etienne in the European Cup, courtesy of substitute David Fairclough's late goal. The gates to Anfield were closed more than an hour before kick-off, and an estimated 10,000 more fans were locked out.

ABOVE: Phil Thompson, 4, beats Kevin Keegan to get the final touch on Liverpool's goal in the 1–1 UEFA Cup semi-final 1–1 draw against Barcelona

ANFIELD'S SUPERSIZED GATES: FIVE HIGHEST (EUROPE)

Opposition	Date	Competition	Attendance
Barcelona	14/4/1976	UEFA Cup (semi-final)	55,104
St. Etienne	16/3/1977	European Cup	55,043
Honved	8/3/1966	Cup Winners' Cup	54,631
Celtic	19/4/1966	Cup Winners' Cup (semi-final)	54,208
Inter Milan	4/5/1965	European Cup (semi-final)	54,082

PREMIER LEAGUE POSSE

Liverpool's five highest home gates of the Premier League era all came in the 2011–12 season. The biggest was for the visit of England's wealthiest club who were on their way to winning their first title in 44 years. A crowd of 45,071 watched the Reds hold Manchester City to a 1–1 draw.

BELOW: Liverpool and Manchester City play out a 1–1 draw in front of Anfield's biggest-ever Premiership crowd

ANFIELD'S SUPERSIZED GATES: FIVE HIGHEST (PREMIER LEAGUE)

Opposition	Date	Attendance
Manchester City	27/11/2011	45,071
Manchester United	15/10/2011	45,065
Sunderland	13/8/2011	45,018
Queens Park Rangers	10/12/2011	45,016
Swansea	5/11/2011	45,013

►► NO ROOM AT THE CAMP NOU

Wembley finals aside, Liverpool drew their biggest-ever crowd on 5 April 2001, when they met Barcelona in a UEFA Cup semi-final, first leg. A total of 90,832 were in the Camp Nou to see the visitors earn a 0–0 draw. In the second leg a Gary McAllister penalty separated the sides and sent Liverpool into the final.

FIVE HIGHEST AWAY ATTENDANCES (LEAGUE)

Opposition	Date	Attendance
Everton	18/9/1948	78,299
Man United	23/3/2008	76,000
Man United	22/10/2006	75,828
Man United	14/3/2009	75,569
Man United	13/1/2013	75,501

FIVE HIGHEST AWAY ATTENDANCES (EUROPE)

Opposition	Date	Competition	Attendance
Barcelona	5/4/2001	UEFA Cup (semi-final)	90,832
Dinamo Tblisi	3/10/1979	European Cup	90,000
Barcelona	21/2/2007	Champions League	88,000
Benfica	1/3/1978	European Cup	80,000
Inter Milan	12/5/1965	European Cup (semi-final)	76,601

ABOVE: Jamie Carragher gets the better of Barcelona's Rivaldo in the goalless 2001 UEFA Cup semi-final second leg, watched by 90,832 fans – the most ever to see Liverpool in a two-legged European tie

ALL EYES ON GOODISON

Due to Manchester United's ground capacity, it's unsurprising that Liverpool's recent visits have drawn some of the biggest English League gates in history. But until Old Trafford undergoes yet another expansion, Liverpool's record away attendance, set on 18 September 1948, looks set to stay. The venue was Goodison Park, scene of the first Merseyside derby of the season, and a crowd of 78,299. The Blues were lying bottom of the First Division at the time but, in true derby tradition, form meant nothing: Everton went ahead from a penalty, and the Reds escaped with a draw thanks to a late equaliser.

Goodison has undergone many alterations and modifications in the last 65 years, and its capacity is now limited to 38,000. This remains its highest attendance for any match, and is unlikely ever to be beaten.

RIGHT: On level terms. Fernando Torres scored Liverpool's equaliser in the Reds' 4–1 away victory over Manchester United in 2009

HISTORY REPEATING

Many things can change over six decades but not the interest and excitement created by a Liverpool–Manchester United FA Cup clash. In January 1948, United entertained the Reds in a Fourth Round 'home' tie at Goodison Park – chosen as the venue because Old Trafford was still being rebuilt after wartime bomb damage. Although 15,000 people were reportedly locked out, 74,721 did manage to get in to watch United win 3–0.

Still, the result was no disgrace. Bob Paisley, who was in the Liverpool side that afternoon, later recalled: 'The United of that time were one of the best teams I ever played against – and they played particularly well that day. Apart from all their other qualities they had the benefit of maturity. I'm sure such a side would have shone in any era.'

That record gate for an FA Cup away tie stood until January 2011, when the two teams met again in the Third Round. The Old Trafford crowd? 74,727 – a mere six more than attended 63 years earlier. Sadly for Liverpool, the outcome was the same. In the opening match of Kenny Dalglish's second managerial reign they were sunk by a second minute penalty.

Although the two gates were almost identical, one thing that definitely changed was the amount of money made. Whilst the 2011 tie generated millions in ticket sales, the official receipts for the earlier Goodison match were £8,810.

LEFT: Face in the crowd. Dalglish's first match back in charge brought 74,727 to Old Trafford

BELOW: Striker David N'gog evades Arsenal's Mikael Silvestre in front of more than 60,000 at the Emirates

FIVE HIGHEST AWAY ATTENDANCES (CUP COMPETITIONS)*

Opposition	Date	Ground	Attendance
Man United	9/1/2011	Old Trafford	74,727
Man United	24/1/1948	Goodison Park	74,721
Everton	29/1/1955	Goodison Park	72,000
Man City	18/2/1956	Maine Road	70,640
Everton	11/3/1967	Goodison Park	64,851

* Chart excludes semi-finals held at neutral grounds. The semis against Burnley (1947) and Everton (1950) were played at Maine Road, Manchester, and both attracted 72,000 fans. The 2012 semi against Everton at Wembley was watched by a crowd of 87,231.

LEAGUE CUP HIGHS – HOME AND AWAY

On 12 February 1980, Nottingham Forest visited Anfield for the second leg of the League Cup semi-final. 50,880 people came to watch Bob Paisley's Champions of England take on Brian Clough's Champions of Europe. It was football's modest and 'quiet man', versus the game's loudest, brashest and self-confessed 'big head'.

Two years earlier, Forest had beaten the Reds in the final of the same competition. So, for Paisley, it was a chance to avenge defeat and prove that he, not Clough, remained British football's top boss. The eagerly anticipated showdown attracted a record Anfield crowd for the tournament, but most went home disappointed. David Fairclough's solitary goal earned a 1–1 draw on the night, but it wasn't enough to cancel the 1–0 deficit from the first leg.

The highest crowd for a League Cup away match came 29 years later, when Liverpool travelled to Arsenal in the Fourth Round. Rafa Benitez's men went down 2–1, in front of 60,004 spectators at the Emirates Stadium.

▼ PLENTY OF SPACE AVAILABLE...

The newly-formed Liverpool FC attracted just 200 fans for their first-ever Lancashire League match at Anfield – a bitter disappointment for founder John Houlding, but hardly a surprise. On the same afternoon his team prepared to face Higher Walton, his old club Everton were kicking off their top-flight Football League programme at home to Nottingham Forest. Faced with the choice, the paying spectators of Merseyside opted for the team they knew, and the superior competition. An estimated 14,000 of them turned up at Goodison.

At least those who chose Anfield got value for their one-penny admission fee, as Liverpool won the match 8–0. But that attendance on 3 September 1892, remains the lowest for any competitive first-team home game. The return fixture seven weeks later attracted only 150 spectators – the fewest ever recorded for a Liverpool away match.

LOWEST HOME GATES – DOMESTIC MATCHES

Competition	Opposition	Date	Attendance
Lancashire League	Higher Walton	3/9/1892	200
Football League (Div 2)	Loughborough Town	7/12/1895	1,000
Football League (Div 1)	Sunderland	30/3/1903	3,000
FA Cup	Burton Swifts	30/1/1897	4,000
League Cup	Brentford	25/10/1983	9,902
Premiership	QPR	8/12/1993	24,561

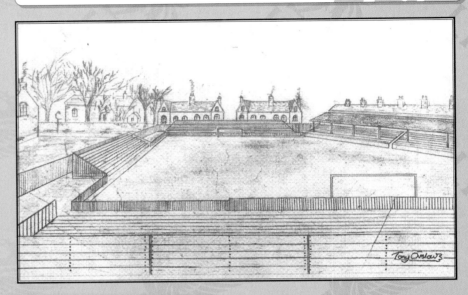

ABOVE: An artist's impression of how Anfield would have looked in 1892

LEFT: Club founder John Houlding could only attract a handful of spectators to the first match – but attendances began to build soon afterwards

DEPRESSION ON THE TERRACES

Like other big clubs, Liverpool enjoyed an attendance boom after World War I, with crowds remaining healthy for more than a decade. But as the Great Depression took hold, they tumbled. Four of the five smallest home League gates between the wars were recorded in the 1930s – the lowest of all on 15 April 1931 when just 6,045 paid to watch a 0–0 draw with Birmingham.

Fifty years later, Britain – and particularly Merseyside – suffered a deep and prolonged recession which hit gates again. Despite winning a League, European and League Cup treble in the 1983–84 season, Liverpool recorded their lowest post-war season attendance while in the top flight. The average home League crowd was 32,021.

LOWEST AWAY GATES – EUROPEAN MATCHES

Competition	Opposition	Date	Attendance
UEFA Cup	Kosice	15/9/1998	4,500
Cup Winners' Cup	Mypa 47	12/9/1996	4,767
European Cup	HJK Helsinki	19/10/1982	5,722
Inter-City Fairs Cup	Dundalk	30/9/1969	6,000

▶▶ DARKNESS BEFORE DAWN

Bill Shankly may have brought the fans to Anfield in record numbers, but his teams weren't always so popular. In 1960–61 – his first full season in charge – home gates fell to an all-time post-war low, with an average of 29,602 passing through the turnstiles for each League match. Liverpool's last home game against Stoke City drew a crowd of only 13,389. Things changed quickly, though. One year later, almost to the day, 40,410 were inside the ground to watch Shankly's men beat Southampton, and clinch promotion to Division One.

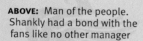

ABOVE: Man of the people. Shankly had a bond with the fans like no other manager

BELOW: Teenage prodigy Robbie Fowler scored a hat-trick in record time – it's a pity so few were at Anfield to see it

LOWEST HOME GATES – EUROPEAN MATCHES

Competition	Opposition	Date	Attendance
European Cup	Dundalk	28/9/1982	12,021
Cup Winners' Cup	Apollon Limassol	16/9/1992	12,769
UEFA Cup	Swarowski Tirol	11/12/1991	16,007
Inter-City Fairs Cup	Dundalk	16/9/1969	32,656

◀◀ LOOK WHAT THEY ALL MISSED....

The 1994–95 season brought Liverpool's lowest home attendances of the Premiership era, with an average of 34,176 per game. The match against Arsenal on 28 August 1994 attracted only 30,017 – the fewest for an opening home League fixture since World War II. But those who turned up saw history being made, as Robbie Fowler hit a hat-trick in just 4 minutes and 32 seconds.

There's no record of how many Liverpool fans made the trip to Nantwich for an FA Cup qualifier back in 1892, although, as the club had only started playing a month earlier, it was presumably very few. Not many home supporters turned up either: the crowd was just 700, according to newspapers of the time. Those who did make the journey would have seen a 4–0 victory to the visitors, including three goals in the space of 10 minutes from striker John Miller. It was the first ever hat-trick by a Liverpool player.

GED THE RED

Liverpool have twice been drawn against the Irish side Dundalk in European competition – and both ties have produced record low attendances. In 1982, the teams met in the European Cup second round. But with the Reds already 4–1 up from the first leg, only 12,769 could be bothered to watch them finish the job at Anfield.

In 1969, the clubs were drawn against each other in the Inter-City Fairs Cup – forerunner of the UEFA Cup. Liverpool's 10–0 victory drew the lowest home crowd for that competition. One of the 32,656 who did make the effort was youthful French schoolteacher – and future LFC manager – Gerard Houllier.

LOWEST AWAY GATES – DOMESTIC MATCHES

Competition	Opposition	Date	Attendance
Lancashire League	Higher Walton	22/10/1892	150
Football League (Div 2)	Rotherham Town	6/1/1894	500
FA Cup	Nantwich	15/10/1892	700
Football League (Div 1)	Notts County	20/4/1907	1,000
League Cup	Luton Town	24/10/1960	6,125
Premiership	Wimbledon	16/1/1993	11,294

ABOVE: The original uncovered Kop was a huge bank of cinders and rubble, separated from the pitch by a wooden fence

PACKING THEM IN AT WEMBLEY

The record number of people to attend a Liverpool match is 100,000. The figure has been reached on 11 occasions, all of them at the old Wembley before ground alterations lowered its capacity.

The six-figure attendances were for the FA Cup finals in 1950, 1965, 1971, 1974 and 1977, and for the League Cup finals in 1978, 1981, 1982, 1983, and 1984. The last occasion was the 1984 Charity Shield match against Everton.

Liverpool's other Wembley finals have attracted the following official attendances:

98,203 (1988 FA Cup final v Wimbledon)
98,000 (1986 FA Cup final v Everton)
96,000 (1987 League Cup final v Arsenal)
92,000 (1978 European Cup final v FC Bruges)
89,102 (2012 FA Cup final v Chelsea)
82,800 (1989 FA Cup final v Everton)
79,544 (1992 FA Cup final v Sunderland)
79,007 (1996 FA Cup final v Manchester United)
75,595 (1995 League Cup final v Bolton Wanderers)

◀◀ GROWING SUPPORT

Although Anfield crowds were low in Liverpool's early Lancashire League days, attendances grew rapidly as they began challenging for promotion and honours. Big FA Cup matches proved a huge draw, with 18,000 paying to see a Round Two tie against the mighty Preston North End in February in 1894.

By the 1894–95 season, with the team in Division One, there were home gates of 20,000 for the visits of Aston Villa, Sunderland and Preston. The 30,000 barrier was broken in a League match with Everton on 21 November 1896. A decade on – with the giant Kop embankment in place – the same fixture attracted the first 40,000 crowd.

It wasn't until February 1920, when the Reds drew Birmingham City in an FA Cup Fourth round tie, that Anfield recorded a 50,000 attendance. Fourteen years later, another Cup clash – this time with Merseyside neighbours Tranmere Rovers – brought more than 60,000 to the ground for the first time.

PREMIER LEAGUE – HOME ATTENDANCE AVERAGES

1992–93	37,009
1993–94	38,503
1994–95	34,175
1995–96	39,552
1996–97	39,776
1997–98	40,628
1998–99	43,321
1999–2000	44,073
2000–01	43,698
2001–02	43,389
2002–03	43,242
2003–04	42,677
2004–05	42,586
2005–06	44,236
2006–07	43,561
2007–08	43,532
2008–09	43,611
2009–10	42,889
2010–11	42,820
2011–12	44,253
2012–13	44,748

BELOW: Kenny Dalglish (in kit as player-manager) and Howard Kendall lead out the Merseyside giants before the 1986 FA Cup final

► CROWDED CARDIFF

The Reds played five finals at the Millennium Stadium while Wembley was being rebuilt. The highest crowd – 74,500 – was for the 2003 League Cup win against Manchester United. The lowest – 71,140 – was for the 2006 FA Cup penalty shoot-out victory over West Ham.

RIGHT: Liverpool fans celebrate the defeat of Manchester United in the 2003 League Cup final

ROGER AND OUT

Supporters have turned out in huge numbers to say goodbye to their Anfield heroes. Nearly 40,000 were at Bill Shankly's testimonial match in 1975, while 35,000 were there to thank Tommy Smith for his years of service in 1977.

But the biggest send-off was reserved for Roger Hunt, the striker whose goals were responsible for so much of the club's success during the 1960s. By April 1972, Hunt had actually been gone for more than two years, seeing out the last of his playing days with Bolton. But when Liverpool agreed to stage a benefit – between the Reds' 1965 FA Cup winning side and an England XI – an incredible 55,214 paid to watch.

The attendance remains a record for a testimonial at Anfield, and stands as a tribute to one of the club's greatest figures. The result? Liverpool 8, England 6 – with Hunt getting a hat-trick.

▼ FROM PALACE...TO PALACE

Liverpool's first ever FA Cup final – the 2–0 defeat to Burnley in 1914 – was also the last to be staged at the old Crystal Palace ground in south London. Among the official crowd of 72,778 was King George V – the first reigning monarch to attend a final and present the medals.

FRIENDLY FANS

In July 2011, Liverpool finished their summer tour of Asia with a 6–3 win over a Malaysian national XI in Kuala Lumpur. The crowd of 85,000 was the highest ever for an LFC pre-season friendly.

The record gate for a pre-season home friendly was set on 30 July 2002, when 44,677 fans witnessed a 1–0 loss to the Italian side, Lazio. That match came 69 years after Anfield hosted its first friendly involving a club from mainland Europe. Rapid Vienna were the visitors in January 1933, going down to a 5–2 defeat in front of 20,000 curious spectators.

SUPPORT THROUGH THE SEASONS

The 1972–73 season brought Liverpool's first trophies for seven years, and more than a million people through the Anfield turnstiles. The average home League attendance was 48,103 – more than for any campaign before or since. League gates in the Premier League era have ranged from an an average of 34,175 in the 1994–95 season to a high of 44,748 in the 2012–13 campaign.

LEFT: Any view will do. Supporters find every available vantage point for the 1914 FA Cup final at Crystal Palace

Managers

On 1 June 1 2012, Brendan Rodgers was confirmed as Liverpool's manager – the first Ulsterman to be appointed since John McKenna 110 years earlier. The Anfield job is one of the most coveted in football, but also among the most pressured. Not surprising, given the towering achievements of some of those who've gone before.

▶▶ THE ONE THAT SHANKS MISSED...

In all his time as manager, Bill Shankly was absent from only one game. In January 1965, Liverpool were drawn at home to Stockport County in the FA Cup Fourth Round. As the Reds were champions, and Stockport were then propping up all other 91 Football League clubs, Shankly felt confident enough to miss the tie and go to watch forthcoming European opponents, FC Cologne, instead. But he was wrong. While Shankly was away, Stockport held on for a 1–1 draw at Anfield – one of the most memorable results in their history.

ABOVE: The father of the modern-day Liverpool FC. Bill Shankly took charge in 1959

BELOW: Bob Paisley's nine-year reign at Anfield yielded a record 13 trophies

◀◀ BOB'S HAUL

In terms of trophies won, it's no contest: Bob Paisley is by far the most successful manager in Liverpool's history. During his nine seasons in charge, he won six League Championships, three European Cups, a UEFA Cup and three League Cups. Deservedly, he was named Manager of the Year six times. Only at Liverpool, where a certain other legendary boss casts a giant shadow, could there be any debate over Paisley's position as the 'greatest'. But, judged on silverware alone, there can only be one conclusion.

Bill Shankly, with three League Championships, two FA Cups and a UEFA Cup, has the second largest trophy haul, along with Kenny Dalglish, who collected three League titles plus two FA Cups and one League Cup. Dalglish is the only boss ever to leave Liverpool, then go on to win the title with another club.

ABOVE: Tom Watson, who spent more than 18 years in the Anfield hot seat

LONGEST REIGN

Tom Watson is Liverpool's longest-serving manager, spending 18 years and 26 days in the Anfield hot seat. Appointed when Queen Victoria was on the throne in 1896, he remained boss until the last day of the 1914–15 season when the Football League programme was suspended due to World War I.

Bill Shankly is the third-longest in post, and although he lasted three and a half years less than Watson, he still holds the record for most games as manager. By the time he announced his shock resignation in July 1974, he had been in charge for 783 matches.

Shankly was the first manager to wrest full control of first team affairs from the LFC board. When interviewed for an earlier vacancy in 1951, he was told that the directors reserved the right to scrutinise the boss's team selection and make changes if they wished. Shankly declined to pursue the job, asking the chairman: 'If I don't pick the team, what am I manager of?'

RIGHT: Roy Hodgsons reign lasted little more than six months

SHORTEST REIGN

With just six months and eight days in charge, Roy Hodgson holds the record for the shortest managerial reign. Unsurprisingly, his total of 31 games in charge is also the lowest. His spell with LFC began on 1 July 2010, and ended by mutual consent on 8 January 2011.

MANAGERIAL LEAGUE TABLE

No man made the Anfield crowd roar like Bill Shankly, and no manager made them roar as often. Shanks delivered 407 wins, more than any other boss before or since. His teams also scored 1,307 goals: that's 87 more than the sides fielded by Tom Watson, and 352 more than Bob Paisley's men. However, he was in charge for more games than either of them.

True performance comparisons are problematic because of the difference in number of matches, standard of competition and strength of opponents. Raw statistics also don't take into account a range of other factors like the state of the squad each manager inherited, the money they had available for transfers, or improvement (or deterioration) over time. One way of assessing relative managerial performance is to look at the number of victories per games played – although, for some, this is equally controversial!

MOST SUCCESSFUL MANAGERS

Manager	P	W	D	L	Win Percentage
McKenna/Barclay	127	77	20	30	60.63
Kenny Dalglish	381	223	94	64	58.53
Bob Paisley	535	308	131	96	57.50
Rafael Benitez	350	197	74	79	56.29
Joe Fagan	131	71	36	24	54.20
Gerard Houllier	307	160	73	74	52.12
Bill Shankly	783	407	198	178	51.98
Roy Evans	226	117	56	53	51.77
Phil Taylor	150	76	32	42	50.67
David Ashworth	139	70	40	29	50.36
Brendan Rodgers	54	25	15	14	46.30
Tom Watson	742	329	141	272	44.34
Graeme Souness	157	66	45	46	42.04
Roy Hodgson	31	13	8	10	41.94
Matt McQueen	229	93	60	76	40.61
George Kay	357	142	93	122	39.78
Evans/Houllier	18	7	6	5	38.89
George Patterson	366	137	85	144	37.43
Don Welsh	232	81	58	93	34.91

ABOVE: Ulsterman John McKenna was Liverpool FC's first manager

BELOW: A proud day for assistant manager Ronnie Moran as he leads the team out at Wembley for the 1992 FA Cup final

◀ THE FIRST BOSS

Liverpool's first-ever manager was John McKenna, an Ulsterman who went on to become one of the game's guiding lights. Although one of two men carrying the title 'club secretary', McKenna was in charge of team matters, while his partner William E. Barclay concentrated on administration. McKenna joined the Everton board in 1887 and was one of a handful of members who stayed loyal to chairman John Houlding when his old club left Anfield for Goodison Park in 1892. When Houlding set up an entirely new club – Liverpool FC – he asked McKenna to give up his job as a health authority vaccinations officer to join him full-time.

McKenna masterminded the trips to Scotland to recruit the so-called 'Team of the Macs' that went on to win the Lancashire League in their first season. He drafted Liverpool's successful application to join the Football League, and won promotion from the Second Division at the first attempt. In 1896, after landing another Division Two championship, McKenna persuaded Tom Watson to move from Sunderland, willingly handing over the managerial reins to the three-time League title winner.

He then became the club's driving commercial force, overseeing all transfer dealings and boosting Anfield's capacity by authorising the building of the Spion Kop. He stayed with the club until 1922, enjoying two spells as chairman, and retained the Football League presidency until his death in 1936.

KENNY – ONE OF A KIND

Kenny Dalglish was the first player-manager in English top-flight football, and the only one in Liverpool's history. As well as being the first player-manager to win an FA Cup, he's the only one to guide a team to the League Championship.

▼ FILLING IN

Ronnie Moran holds the distinction of leading out a Liverpool team for a Wembley final, despite not being the boss. In May 1992, he was coming to the end of his spell as 'caretaker manager', brought about by Graeme Souness's heart surgery. During his month in the chair, he oversaw seven League games plus the FA Cup semi-final against Portsmouth which the Reds won on penalties.

It was Moran's second stint as caretaker. A year earlier he was asked to take charge of first-team affairs for the 10 matches between the resignation of Kenny Dalglish and the arrival of Souness.

PHIL'S REGRET

Phil Taylor is the only Liverpool boss never to have managed a team in the top flight. A former player in the first post-war Championship-winning side, Taylor was appointed in 1956, two years after the team's relegation. He spent three seasons trying to revive their fortunes but, although they never finished outside the top four of the Second Division under his command, they weren't quite good enough to win promotion.

In November 1959, with the team lying in mid-table, an exhausted Taylor explained his decision to step down: 'No matter how great has been the disappointment of the directors at our failure to win our way back to the First Division, it has not been greater than mine. I made it my goal. I set my heart on it and strove for it with all the energy I could muster. Such striving has not been enough, and now the time has come to hand over to someone else to see if they can do better.'

A fortnight later, the board appointed Bill Shankly.

ABOVE: Phil Taylor (back row, far left) with the team that were never quite good enough to win promotion

DOUBLE ACTS

The appointment of Roy Evans and Gerard Houllier as joint managers in 1998 meant, for the first time in almost a century, Liverpool had two men officially in charge of the team. But, whereas the first experiment involving John McKenna and W. E. Barclay proved to be a success lasting four years, this partnership lasted a mere three months. After 18 games in joint-charge Evans departed, leaving Houllier to get on with the job on his own.

RIGHT: Failed experiment. The joint-managerial reign of Roy Evans and Gerard Houllier was short-lived

YOUNG AND OLD

When Bob Paisley took his team to Watford on the final day of the 1982–83 season – his last match in charge – he was 64 years, three months and three weeks old. Among his many records, he's the oldest manager in LFC's history. Paisley was 56 when he took over the reins from Bill Shankly, making him the fifth oldest to be appointed. Brendan Rodgers is one of the youngest managers in the Premier League but, at 39, he took the job at a more advanced age than several of his predecessors.

YOUNGEST APPOINTMENTS

Manager	Age
Kenny Dalglish (first term)	34
John McKenna	37 years, 2 months
Tom Watson	37 years, 3 months
Graeme Souness	37 years, 10 months
Phil Taylor	38

OLDEST APPOINTMENTS

Manager	Age
Roy Hodgson	63
Joe Fagan	62
Kenny Dalglish (second term)	59 years, 10 months
Matt McQueen	59 years, 8 months
Bob Paisley	56

ABOVE: Job Done! Joe Fagan relaxes after delivering the European Cup in his first season in charge in 1984

JOE'S INCREDIBLE TREBLE

In 1984, Joe Fagan became the first post-war boss in England to win the League Championship in his first year of management: a feat equalled by Kenny Dalglish, who did it two years later. As well as lifting the League Cup, Joe also went on to win the European Cup in Rome – an achievement only matched by Pep Guardiola who led Barcelona to Champions League success in 2009, just 12 months after taking charge.

Joe's break into management came after 25 years on the coaching staff. At 62, he only ever intended to do the job for two full seasons. Sadly, while the first one finished with an historic treble-winning triumph, his second ended in the tragedy of Heysel.

SWAPPING KIT FOR SUIT

Six LFC managers have previously played for the club. Matt McQueen was the first, taking charge in 1923, almost 24 years after his last appearance on the pitch. McQueen was part of the original Liverpool team, and was in the line-up for their first-ever match in the Football League. After retiring he became a referee, although he later returned to Anfield as a director.

His first three months in the hot seat could hardly have gone better. He oversaw the final 14 First Division matches of the season, and guided the team to their second successive League title. Unfortunately, McQueen never managed more than a fourth place finish for the rest of his time in charge. In 1928, after losing a leg in a horrific car crash, he decided to call it a day.

FROM LFC PLAYER...TO LFC BOSS
Matt McQueen
Phil Taylor
Bob Paisley
Kenny Dalglish
Graeme Souness
Roy Evans

BELOW: George Kay, the Mancunian who dedicated himself to Liverpool – and won the League title

GEORGE THE FIRST...

With his eight barren seasons in charge, George Patterson is the manager to go the longest period without a trophy. The former club secretary took over in 1928, and although he kept the team in Division One, he never managed to make a serious challenge for honours. In his last season he narrowly escaped relegation, and both he and the board agreed he should return to administrative duties.

Despite his lack of silverware, Patterson brought some influential players to the club, including captain – and future Manchester United legend – Matt Busby. In 1930, he splashed out £8,000 on the giant Bury centre-back Tom 'Tiny' Bradshaw, setting a club-record transfer fee that wouldn't be beaten for another 16 years.

...AND GEORGE THE SECOND

George Kay's 15-year spell as Liverpool boss was interrupted by World War II. But when the fighting was over he set about rebuilding a team that would go on to win the first post-war League Championship. Three years later he led the Reds to Wembley for the first time in 36 years, although that trip to face Arsenal in the 1950 FA Cup final ended in defeat.

As well as landing the League title, Kay will be remembered for some of the players he brought to Anfield. His most notable capture came in 1946 when he smashed the club transfer record to sign Newcastle striker Albert Stubbins for £12,500. Less eye-catching, but with far more important long-term consequences, was his recruitment of two youngsters shortly before the outbreak of the war: Billy Liddell and Bob Paisley.

AN UNWISE MOVE

Few managers would willingly walk out on a team that's top of the table. Even fewer would leave them for a club that's heading for relegation. In 1923, manager David Ashworth did just that. With Liverpool on course for their second Championship under his guidance, he stunned the board by resigning and moving to one of his former clubs, Oldham Athletic, who had made him a 'lucrative offer' to return. Perhaps they regretted it afterwards. As Liverpool ended the 1922–23 season as Champions, Oldham went down to Division Two, making Ashworth the only English manager to win the League title and then be relegated in successive seasons.

SUCCESS AWAY FROM ANFIELD

In 1896, Tom Watson arrived at Anfield as the most celebrated manager in the country. In the space of six seasons he'd won three League Championships with Sunderland. Until 2010, when Kenny Dalglish resumed control following his Premiership success at Blackburn, no other Liverpool manager had lifted the English League title with another club.

Graeme Souness was the first boss to have tasted League success outside England, having already led Glasgow Rangers to three Scottish championships. Gerard Houllier had won a League title in France, while Rafa Benitez had won two in Spain. By the time Roy Hodgson joined Liverpool he had managed in eight different countries, including Sweden, where he won seven League titles with two different clubs.

ABOVE: David Ashworth, who cut short his Anfield career while it was at its height

BELOW: Player and manager. Souness returned as boss after a glittering career as skipper

Stadiums

The word "iconic" is much overused, but in the case of Anfield Stadium – the only home Liverpool FC has ever known – iconic is entirely appropriate. Anyone who has ever witnessed a match there will agree, especially one those tensely atmospheric European nights, Anfield is a very special place.

VISITORS WELCOME

Apart from football, Anfield has staged a number of other events, including basketball, tennis, boxing bouts and rugby league internationals. It's also hosted rock concerts – and even a weeklong series of mass prayer meetings held by the American evangelist Billy Graham in 1984. The biggest single attendance for a non-football event at Anfield is believed to be in 1938 when an estimated crowd of more than 40,000 watched Lancashire-born boxer Peter Kane beat Jackie Jurich to win the World Flyweight title.

UP ON THE BIG SCREEN

Anfield once attracted a crowd of 40,149 – for a match that wasn't even played there. When the Reds were drawn against Everton in a 1967 Fifth Round FA Cup tie, demand for tickets at Goodison Park was so great that the club decided to show the match live on eight giant CCTV screens inside their own ground. Tickets sold out within 36 hours, leading to a record combined gate of 105,000.

WHY 'THE KOP'?

The Kop takes its name from 'Spioenkop', a hill in South Africa's Natal province, and scene of one of the Boer War's bloodiest battles, in which 320 men from the Lancashire Fusiliers were killed. Ernest Edwards, long-time football correspondent of the *Liverpool Echo*, suggested that LFC name their giant new embankment in memory of the fallen. After chairman John McKenna agreed, several other clubs opened similar 'kops' at their grounds.

▼ FLAGPOLE CORNER

The flagpole at the corner of the Kop and Centenary Stand is the topmast of Isambard Kingdom Brunel's SS *Great Eastern*, which, on her launch in 1858, was the biggest sea-going vessel in the world. After finishing transatlantic service, she sailed up and down the Mersey bedecked with advertising hoardings for the city's largest department store, Lewis's. After the ship was broken up in Birkenhead, the LFC board bought the flagpole for 20 guineas, and transported it across the Mersey, first by ferry to Garston, then by a team of horse-drawn carriages to Anfield.

BELOW: 'Flagpole Corner' was a popular meeting place for fans even a century ago

▶▶ THE ANFIELD STORY

Although synonymous with Liverpool, Anfield was originally home to Everton FC who played there for eight seasons before their move to Goodison Park. Their first match at the newly built ground was on 27 September 1884, when they beat Earlestown 5–0. Eight years later the Everton directors voted to quit in a dispute over rent – leaving their landlord and former chairman, John Houlding, with a stadium, but no team.

Houlding set about forming a new club – Liverpool FC – which gained entry to the Lancashire League. On 1 September 1892, two days before the season started, his hastily assembled team played their first match at Anfield: a friendly against Rotherham Town which they won 7–1.

Anfield has staged thousands of matches since then, from League games and FA Cup ties to internationals and even European finals. It's become world-famous for its unique atmosphere, generated largely by the vast Spion Kop terrace, built in 1906 and initially comprised of nothing more than cinders and rubble. In 1928 it was reconstructed, fitted with 100 concrete steps, extended to house 28,000 spectators, and topped with a 45,000 square-feet roof, making it the largest covered terrace in Europe. The modern-day Kop – fitted with seats in 1994 – can accommodate less than half the old amount, but it remains the largest single-tier structure in Britain.

At 45,520, Anfield currently has the sixth largest capacity in the Premier League, although there are plans to redevelop the ground and boost the number of seats to 60,000.

FIT FOR A KING

In February 1888, Anfield hosted its first FA Cup semi-final, as Preston North End beat Crewe Alexandra 4–0. It's staged four other FA Cup semis since then, including a 1921 tie between Wolves and Cardiff, watched from the Main Stand by King George VI and Queen Elizabeth.

TV FAVOURITES

On 22 August 1964, the BBC broadcast its first-ever *Match of the Day* programme from Anfield, as Liverpool beat Arsenal 3–2. As it was shown on BBC2, which was then only available in the London area, the programme attracted just 20,000 viewers – less than half the number inside the ground. On 15 November 1969, the *MotD* cameras were again at Anfield for Liverpool's 2–0 victory over West Ham. It was the first time the programme was broadcast in colour.

▼ RAIN STOPS PLAY

Of all the European finals held on British soil, only one has had to be abandoned – and that was at Anfield. On 9 May 1973, Liverpool took on Borussia Moenchengladbach in the UEFA Cup final first leg – only to be sent back down the tunnel after 25 minutes due to torrential rain and a waterlogged pitch. The match was replayed 24 hours later, with admission prices slashed to 10 pence. Liverpool won 3–0, and went on to lift the trophy in Germany.

BELOW: Rain stops play. A waterlogged Anfield on the night of the 1973 UEFA Cup final, first leg

WINNING IN WALES

The Reds were the first team to lift the League Cup, the FA Cup and the Community Shield at the Millennium Stadium, completing a hat-trick of wins in 2001 – the year the ground became a substitute for Wembley. The League Cup final against Birmingham City was the first club match at the Cardiff stadium, and the Community Shield clash with Manchester United was the first game in the UK to be held under a closed roof.

Liverpool played in a record three League Cup finals in Cardiff, beating United in their second in 2003, but losing to Chelsea in 2005. They also won the last FA Cup and Community Shield finals staged at the ground, running out winners against West Ham and Chelsea in 2006.

Robbie Fowler was the first club player to score at the stadium, getting the first goal against Birmingham in 2001. The last to score was Peter Crouch, who hit the winner in the 2–1 Community Shield victory over Chelsea.

BELOW: The first of many. Robbie Fowler with the 2001 League Cup – won at Cardiff's Millennium Stadium

BRUM, HERE WE COME

Liverpool have won four FA Cup semi-finals at Villa Park – and gone on to lift the trophy after each of them. Their first success came in 1965 when a crowd of more than 67,000 saw them beat Chelsea 2–0 en route to their first ever Wembley triumph. The Reds beat Leicester City in a replayed semi in 1974, despatched Portsmouth on penalties in 1992, and saw off Wycombe Wanderers on their way to the Treble in 2001.

Villa Park was also the scene of the club's first ever League Cup success. On 1 April 1981, two weeks after West Ham had denied them at Wembley with a goal in the last minute of extra time, the teams met in Birmingham for the replay. A young Ian Rush announced himself as a future star that Wednesday night with a brilliant display. But it was goals from Kenny Dalglish and Alan Hansen that sealed a 2–1 win and ensured that Liverpool were presented with the Cup.

◀◀ 'ANFIELD SOUTH'

Liverpool were such frequent visitors to the national stadium during their years of peak success that, for many fans, Wembley really did feel like a second home. In fact from 1965 to 1996 the team made an incredible 30 appearances. That included nine FA Cup finals, seven League Cup finals, one European Cup final and 13 Charity Shields.

The old Wembley was closed in 2000, demolished soon afterwards and then rebuilt in time for the 2007 FA Cup final. It was another five years before Liverpool made their first appearance, beating Cardiff City to lift the League Cup. Two months later they were back for a meeting with Everton in the FA Cup semis. Victory led to a third, but unsuccessful, appearance as they were beaten in the final by Chelsea.

WOLVES BITTEN

At least 20,000 Liverpudlians made the Tuesday night trip to Molineux for the last League game of the 1975–76 season. For both sides a win was essential. Liverpool needed it to clinch the Championship, and only maximum points would save Wolves from certain relegation. The home side scored early in the first half and held onto their slender lead until the final dramatic 15 minutes when Kevin Keegan levelled and John Toshack put the Reds ahead. Ray Kennedy settled matters in the final minute, sparking a mass pitch invasion and unforgettable celebrations to mark Bob Paisley's first-ever League title as manager. Back on Merseyside, Elton John announced the result to a packed Liverpool Empire – before leading the audience in a mass sing-along of 'You'll Never Walk Alone'.

OLD TRAFFORD, OLD ADVERSARY

Liverpool were the first-ever visitors to Old Trafford, beating Manchester United 4–3 in the inaugural League match on 19 February 1910. As well as countless epic battles with their north-west rivals since then, the Reds have played five FA Cup semi-finals at the ground – the first in 1971 when they won 2–1 against Everton, and the last in 2006 when they beat Chelsea by the same score. The stadium also hosted the replay of Liverpool's first League Cup final, which they lost to Nottingham Forest in 1978.

THE MAINE MEN

Two all-Merseyside FA Cup semi-finals were held at Manchester City's old Maine Road ground. Liverpool won the first in 1950, and the second in 1977 – although that one had to go to a replay. Liverpool and Everton also replayed the 1984 League Cup final at the stadium after the Wembley match ended in a 0–0 stalemate. The Reds were victorious again, thanks to a first-half strike from Graeme Souness.

ABOVE: Mayhem at Molineux. Tommy Smith (left) and Ian Callaghan escape the invading hordes after clinching the Championship in 1976

RIGHT: Tripled Scotch. Left to right, Alan Hansen, Kenny Dalgish and Graeme Souness with the League Cup at Maine Road in 1984

LIVERPOOL'S EUROPEAN FINAL VENUES

1966   Cup Winners' Cup, Hampden Park, Glasgow
1973   UEFA Cup 2nd Leg, Bokelberg, Moenchengladbach
1976   UEFA Cup 2nd Leg, Olympic Stadium, Bruges
1977   European Cup, Stadio Olimpico, Rome
1978   European Cup, Wembley Stadium, London
1981   European Cup, Parc des Princes, Paris
1984   European Cup, Stadio Olimpico, Rome
1985   European Cup, Heysel Stadium, Brussels
2001   UEFA Cup, Westfalenstadion, Dortmund
2005   UEFA Champions League, Ataturk Stadium, Istanbul
2007   UEFA Champions League, Olympic Stadium, Athens

 TURKISH DELIGHT

Just as a certain generation will never forget Rome in 1977, younger fans will find the memories of Istanbul in 2005 impossible to erase. The venue for Liverpool's extraordinary Champions League final comeback against AC Milan was the Ataturk Stadium, a vast sunken bowl 12 miles from the city centre. The official crowd that night was 65,000, the largest ever for a match involving a non-Turkish side at the stadium. Since the final, the Ataturk has become home to Turkey's Super Lig club Istanbul BB. In 2011, reconstruction work started to boost the capacity to 90,000. By the time of the Euro 2016 championships it will be the world's largest stadium with every seat under cover.

 ROME

The Stadio Olimpico in Rome was the scene of two of Liverpool's European Cup finals. The first in 1977 marked the ultimate triumph for a club that had been competing on the continent for 13 consecutive seasons. An estimated 25,000 travelling fans – thought to be the biggest mass migration of club supporters up to that point – watched their team record an historic 3–1 victory over Borussia Moenchengladbach.

Liverpool returned seven years later to face AS Roma – the club that called the stadium home. Incredibly, UEFA refused all requests to change the allotted venue once the Italian champions had reached the final. So, the Kopites headed to Italy once more, this time with their ticket allocation cut to just 12,000. The rest of the ground was taken up with Roma's own fans who watched in disbelief and anger as their team lost on penalties.

UEFA later ruled that if the same circumstances ever arose, the final would be switched to neutral territory. This would be the last time a team could compete in the last stage of Europe's premier competition on their own ground.

ABOVE: One night in Istanbul. Liverpool fans in full voice before the 2005 UEFA Champions League final

BELOW: Into the lions' den. Graeme Souness leads his men into the cauldron of Rome's Stadio Olimpico in 1984

ABOVE: Let battle commence. The start of the second leg of the 1973 UEFA Cup final in Moenchengladbach

EARLY TRAVELLERS

Liverpool's first match outside England was at Ibrox Stadium, Glasgow, on 6 October 1892, when they were beaten 6–1 by Rangers in a friendly. They played their first game in Ireland on 13 April 1903, when they met Bohemians at Dalymount Park in Dublin. In May 1910, the club went on an end of season tour of Scandinavia, playing their first match on mainland Europe at the home of Orgryte IS in Gothenburg, Sweden. Their first competitive match overseas was at Iceland's national stadium, the Laugardalsvollur – formerly used by KR Rejkyavik. Bill Shankly's team beat the Icelandic champions 5–0 in a European Cup preliminary round on 17 August 1964.

▶▶ HEYSEL TRAGEDY

The 1985 European Cup final between Liverpool and Juventus was held at Heysel Stadium, Brussels: a venue that would become infamous in football history. Security arrangements to cope with the 60,000 fans crammed in to the ground were wholly inadequate. Followers of both teams were allocated tickets behind the same goal. There were no police to segregate them, and no stewards to enforce a supposed alcohol ban.

Despite prior assurances from UEFA and the Belgian football authorities that the stadium was safe, it was, in fact, dilapidated. In the hours leading up to the match, turnstiles collapsed, crush barriers came away from the concrete steps, and terraces crumbled beneath spectators' feet. Skirmishes before the kick-off culminated in a charge from the Liverpool section which created a stampede by fleeing Italian fans. In the resulting crush, a wall collapsed causing the deaths of 39 spectators. Following a trial in Belgium, 14 people received three-year sentences for involuntary manslaughter.

As punishment for what happened in Brussels, all English clubs were banned from European competition for five years. Liverpool FC weren't allowed to compete until 1991. Heysel itself was later torn down, rebuilt, and reopened in 1995 as the King Baudouin Stadium.

Today, a plaque in memory of those who died in the disaster remains on permanent display at Anfield.

▶▶ BYE BYE, BOKELBERG

The Bokelberg Stadion in Germany, where Liverpool won their first European silverware, no longer exists. The former home of Borussia Moenchengladbach was demolished in 2006 after the club moved to its new ground, Borussia Park. The site was cleared a year later to make way for a housing estate.

BELOW: An Anfield tribute to those who lost their lives at Heysel Stadium in 1985

STADIUMS – EUROPEAN VENUES   115

Hillsborough

On 15 April 1989, more than 24,000 Liverpool fans attended the FA Cup semi-final against Nottingham Forest at Hillsborough stadium, Sheffield. Ninety-six of those supporters never returned home. All were crushed to death on the Leppings Lane terrace in what became the worst-ever disaster at a British sporting event.

The true causes of the tragedy were, for many years, obscured by press reports which sought to pin the blame on the fans themselves. Those fabricated newspaper stories stemmed from untrue information given out by police in an attempt to deflect attention from their own failings. Two independent inquiries have since cleared the supporters of any responsibility.

COUNTDOWN TO DISASTER

Many Liverpool fans were delayed in getting to Sheffield because of motorway roadworks. Once there, they found they could only enter the ground through a small number of decrepit turnstiles. The combination of late arrivals and slow admission caused a huge build-up of fans outside the stadium in the half-hour before kick-off. In a bid to relieve the congestion a senior policeman ordered the opening of a gate which led thousands of fans directly into a section of the Leppings Lane terrace that was already dangerously overcrowded. The influx put huge pressure on fans at the front of the terrace who were unable to escape due to the perimeter fencing designed to stop pitch invasions. It also put an added strain on the crush barriers, many of which failed to meet proper safety standards. Five minutes after kick-off one of those barriers gave way, causing spectators to fall on top of one other.

CHAOS AND CONFUSION

As the match continued, desperate fans struggled to escape the crush by scaling the perimeter fences. Others were dragged to safety by those in the upper tiers. Initial screams for help were ignored or misunderstood, and it wasn't until 3.06pm that players and officials began to realise what was happening. The referee first suspended and then abandoned the match, but the response from the emergency services was slow and badly co-ordinated. Firefighters with cutting gear had difficulty getting into the ground, and although dozens of ambulances were dispatched, access to the pitch was delayed because police were reporting 'crowd trouble'. In the absence of medical help, some supporters tore up advertising hoardings to use as makeshift stretchers and tried to administer first aid to the injured.

THE TRUTH

An independent inquiry by Lord Justice Taylor later found that a 'failure of police control' was largely responsible for the disaster. In 2012, the Hillsborough Independent Panel, which had been given access to all official documents, stated that crowd safety had been 'compromised at every level'. It found that 116 of 164 witness statements unfavourable to South Yorkshire Police had been removed in an attempt to blame Liverpool fans for the fatal crush. It also revealed that as many as 41 of the victims might have been revived and survived had they been treated more promptly.

In December 2012 the High Court quashed the original inquest verdicts of accidental death, clearing the way for new hearings into exactly how and why the 96 lost their lives.

Miscellaneous

Up until the end of the 20012–13 season, Liverpool had scored 471 penalties, with 75 different players being successful from the spot. The club has been fortunate in having players with cool heads to willingly take on the responsibility. But only a few – like Danny Murphy, who never missed any of his eight penalty kicks – can boast a 100 per cent success rate. Still, others have come close. And their strong nerves, combined with an accuracy from 12 yards, has been critical to the team's success

ALDO'S AGONY

John Aldridge scored 17 penalties for Liverpool, but the one he missed will always haunt him. Dave Beasant's 60th minute save in May 1988 made Aldridge the first player to miss from the spot in a Wembley FA Cup final. It also meant that Wimbledon were able to hold on to a slender 1–0 lead and deliver one of the biggest ever upsets in the tournament's history.

'Aldo' marked his last appearance for the Reds by making more history. With the team already 5–0 up against Crystal Palace, he was brought on as a substitute to take a 67th minute penalty. He raced from the touchline to the spot, converting with his first touch. Liverpool went on to win 9–0, and Aldridge bade farewell by throwing his shirt and boots into the Kop.

ABOVE: Denied by Dave. John Aldridge's penalty kick in the 1988 FA Cup final is saved by Wimbledon's Beasant – it was the only penalty he missed for the Reds

JAN'S THE MAN

Jan Molby is Liverpool's undisputed penalty king. He scored 42 goals from the spot, missing only three times: a 93.3 per cent conversion rate. The big Dane took on the penalty-taking responsibilities early in the 1985–86 season, getting off to a flyer by scoring two in the same match against Tottenham. A year later he went one better, scoring an unprecedented hat-trick of penalties in a League Cup tie against Coventry.

Most keepers had little chance against Molby's fierce shot, but he was also an expert at placing his kicks out of reach. Asked to explain his success from the spot, he later revealed: 'I had a technique that meant I never made my mind up where I was putting it. I would run up, take a look at the goalkeeper and if he moved early, I'd have the nerve to go the other way. And if he didn't dive early I would just put it hard and low to his right.'

BELOW 42 out of 45 isn't bad. Liverpool's penalty king, Jan Molby

TOP PENALTY-TAKERS

Name	Scored	Missed
Jan Molby	42	3
Phil Neal	38	13
Billy Liddell	34	7
Steven Gerrard	31	8
Tommy Smith	22	10
Robbie Fowler	20	6
John Aldridge	17	1
Terry McDermott	16	4
Gordon Hodgson	15	1
Michael Owen	13	10

KEEPING THEIR HEADS

The Reds have become famous for shoot-outs in European finals, but have also relied on penalty-takers – and savers – in normal time.

In the 1973 UEFA Cup final first leg at Anfield, Ray Clemence stopped a penalty by Jupp Heynckes, denying Borussia Moenchengladbach a priceless away goal. Three years later, Kevin Keegan capped a dramatic fight-back in the final of the same competition. His second half spot kick gave the team a 3–2 first leg victory over FC Bruges, after being 0–2 down.

In 1977 it was Phil Neal who kept his cool, this time on an even bigger stage. His 82nd minute penalty in Rome – against Borussia Moenchengladbach once more – effectively sealed Liverpool's first European Cup triumph.

And in 2001, Gary McAllister was on target from the spot as Liverpool drew 4–4 with Alaves – a UEFA Cup final they later went on to win thanks to an extra time 'golden goal'.

ABOVE: Phil Neal slots his 82nd-minute penalty past Wolfgang Kneib to seal the 1977 European Cup victory

RIGHT: Comeback complete. Kevin Keegan's spot-kick in the first leg of the 1976 UEFA Cup final

BILL'S BAD CHOICE

One of the many famous opposition players who missed from the spot at Anfield was Bill Shankly, while a Preston North End player. Goalkeeper Ray Minshull saved his penalty in a 1947 League match that Liverpool went on to win 3–0.

Apparently, Minshull knew what to expect, as Liverpool striker Albert Stubbins later explained in a newspaper column: 'Before our Easter Monday games with Preston Jack Balmer commented that Bill Shankly always placed penalty kicks to the left side of goalkeepers. During the game when Preston were awarded a spot kick, the wily Shankly ran at the ball as though to slam it – instead he attempted a place shot. Ray Minshull was prepared, and his clever save ended any hopes Preston had of saving the game.'

'GOOD SHOT, SIR!'

The first recorded Liverpool player to score a penalty was full-back Duncan McLean in a Division Two home match against Northwich Victoria on 3 February 1894. According to newspaper reports, the referee penalised the visitors when one of their defenders 'palpably fouled the ball within the dreaded twelve-yard limit'. McLean apparently scored 'somewhat easily by shooting over the Northwich custodian's head'.

QUICKEST TO CONVERT

Liverpool's two fastest penalties in the Premier League were both scored in the second minute. Steven Gerrard's spot kick at Stoke on Boxing Day 2012 was awarded for a foul on Luis Suarez after just 37 seconds.

In March 2000, Emile Heskey was brought down in the first minute against Sunderland at Anfield, and Patrik Berger stepped up to convert. It was Heskey's debut for the club, and Berger's 100th League appearance.

THINK PENALTIES ARE UNFAIR?

Before the days of shoot-outs, matches that were level after extra time either went to replays or were decided on the toss of a coin. In 1965, after both Liverpool's second round European Cup ties with FC Cologne ended goalless, the teams played out a 2–2 replay in neutral Rotterdam. Then after 300 minutes of stalemate, the referee flipped a coin and asked the skippers to choose. Ron Yeats called 'tails' – and proved to be right.

Three years later, Liverpool's 2–1 home victory over Atletico Bilbao was enough to cancel out the 1–2 reverse in the first leg. But, with no further goals in extra time, the Fairs Cup clash also had to be settled by a game of chance. This time it was the Spaniards who called it correctly, and the Reds went out. It was the last time a coin toss was used to settle a European club tie. In 1970, FIFA decreed that penalties would be used to break any future stalemates.

THE STORY SO FAR

Liverpool have been involved in 13 shootouts since the match-deciding system was introduced. They were the first club to win the European Cup, the League Cup and the Charity Shield on spot kicks. They were also the first British club to win both European and domestic trophies – and are unique in lifting two European Cups and two League Cups as a result of shoot-outs. Both of Liverpool's two defeats in shoot-outs came in the League Cup. They lost to Wimbledon in a 1993 Fourth Round replay, and to Northampton in a Third Round tie in 2010.

▼ SHOWDOWN IN ROME

Liverpool made history in 1984, beating their opponents Roma on their home turf, and securing their victory in the tournament's first-ever shoot-out. Phil Neal, Graeme Souness, Ian Rush and Alan Kennedy were all on target from the spot, although it was keeper Bruce Grobbelaar who shared equal credit. 'Try to put them off', was the advice from boss, Joe Fagan – and Grobbelaar took it, wobbling his legs, knocking his knees and pretending to eat the netting as each Roma player stepped up. Italian international Bruno Conti was so distracted he placed his kick wide. Roma's star striker Francesco Graziani then blazed his shot over the crossbar – leaving Kennedy to convert the decider.

SIX OF THE BEST AT WEMBLEY

The 1974 Charity Shield against Leeds ended with the first shoot-out in the trophy's history – and the first to be held at Wembley. With the match ending 1–1, Liverpool went into the shoot-out without one of their surest spot-kick takers, Kevin Keegan, who had earlier been sent off. But they needn't have worried. Six players – Alec Lindsay, Emlyn Hughes, Brian Hall, Tommy Smith, Peter Cormack and Ian Callaghan – all converted.

Leeds, whose captain Billy Bremner was dismissed for fighting with Keegan, also scored their first five spot kicks. But, in the absence of their skipper, had to turn to goalkeeper David Harvey to take the sixth. He missed.

BELOW: Bruce Grobbelaar's antics were sufficient to put off two of Roma's penalty-takers in the 1984 European Cup final shootout

THEY SHALL NOT PASS PEPE

Jose Reina holds the record for most penalties saved by a Liverpool keeper in a shoot-out – stopping three out of four in the 2006 FA Cup final. The Reds only went into the penalty decider thanks to the Spaniard denying West Ham victory with a brilliant save in the last minute of normal time. He then went on to save from Bobby Zamora, Paul Konchesky and Anton Ferdinand as Liverpool ran out 6–4 winners. A year later, Reina was also on top form in the Champions League semi-final shoot-out against Chelsea, saving from Geremi and Arjen Robben to help the Reds go through to the final in Athens.

LEFT: Pepe Reina is mobbed by team mates after his vital third save from West Ham's Anton Ferdinand at the 2006 FA Cup final

JERZY COPIES BRUCIE

Bruce Grobbelaar's behaviour in the 1984 European Cup final was the inspiration for Jerzy Dudek's antics in Istanbul 21 years later. The Polish keeper saved brilliantly from AC Milan's Andrea Pirlo and Andriy Shevchenko, but his distraction tactics also caused the Brazilian, Serginho, to miss his shot. Liverpool, who scored from the spot through Dietmar Hamann, Djibril Cisse and Vladimir Smicer, went on to be crowned Champions of Europe for the fifth time.

GERRARD ON THE SPOT

Steven Gerrard has been involved in more penalty shoot-outs than any other Liverpool player – taking part in four during his Anfield career. He scored in three of them: the League Cup tie against Ipswich in 2002, the 2006 FA Cup final against West Ham, and the 2007 Champions League semi-final against Chelsea. His one miss came in the 2012 League Cup final. However, he still ended up on the winning side thanks to another miss from Cardiff City's Anthony Gerrard – his cousin.

RIGHT: Steven Gerrard consoles cousin Anthony whose Wembley penalty miss for Cardiff proved crucial in 2012

IN THE BEGINNING

The FA Charity/Community Shield began in 1908 as a replacement for the Dewar Shield, played at the end of each season between the top sides from England's professional and amateur leagues. The trophy – also known as the Sheriff of London Charity Shield – was more than six feet high and thought to be the largest competed for in the history of football. The competition was devised by the whisky distiller and Conservative MP, Sir Thomas Dewar, as a means of raising money for hospitals and other good causes.

Liverpool took part in the Dewar Shield only once, when as 1906 Football League champions, they played Corinthians at Fulham's Craven Cottage ground in front of a 20,000-strong crowd. 'The club makes nothing out of its meeting today,' reported the *Liverpool Daily Post*. 'They go up to town for the bare railway and hotel expenses.' Nevertheless, it proved to be a worthwhile trip. Liverpool won 5–1 with striker Joe Hewitt netting a hat-trick.

ABOVE: That'll take some lifting. Liverpool's 1906 Championship-winning side with the Dewar Shield

FIRST TROPHY OF THE SEASON

The Reds have made 21 appearances in the Charity (later Community) Shield, winning the trophy outright on 10 occasions, and sharing it a record five times. They took part in the first final to be staged at Wembley, and the first and last matches held at Cardiff's Millennium Stadium. Liverpool have contested the Shield at six venues in all, including Anfield. The match was held there in 1964 when Liverpool, as League Champions, drew 2–2 with FA Cup holders West Ham United. Terry McDermott and Ian Rush are the club's top scorers in the competition, with three goals each.

HIGHS AND LOWS

The record attendance for a Shield match was set in 1984, when Liverpool and Everton attracted 100,000 fans to Wembley. The lowest figure for a Shield final at the old stadium was in 1988 when Liverpool's 2–1 victory over Wimbledon was watched by a crowd of just 54,887.

LEFT: Terry McDermott celebrates his first-half winner against West Ham at the 1980 Charity Shield

FA CHARITY/COMMUNITY SHIELD WON

Year	Opposition	Result	Venue
1966	Everton	1–0	Goodison Park
1974	Leeds United	7–6*	Wembley
1976	Southampton	1–0	Wembley
1979	Arsenal	3–1	Wembley
1980	West Ham United	1–0	Wembley
1982	Tottenham Hotspur	1–0	Wembley
1988	Wimbledon	2–1	Wembley
1989	Arsenal	1–0	Wembley
2001	Manchester United	2–1	Millennium Stadium
2006	Chelsea	2–1	Millennium Stadium

* on penalties

◀◀ SHANKLY'S LAST APPEARANCE

The 1974 Charity Shield was the first to be held at Wembley, the first to be decided on penalties, the first to be televised live, and the first in which players were sent off. It was also the last time that Bill Shankly led Liverpool out. Although he had announced his retirement a month earlier, Shanks was given the honour of being in charge for the season's curtain raiser, and left Wembley with one final trophy under his belt before handing over to Bob Paisley.

LEFT: Bill's farewell. Bill Shankly leads the Reds out for the 1974 Charity Shield, flanked by short-lived Leeds boss, Brian Clough

▶▶ MEETING THE NEIGHBOURS

The Reds have met Everton three times in the Charity Shield – winning, drawing and losing once. In August 1966, more than 63,000 fans turned out to witness history: England's World Cup winners Roger Hunt and Ray Wilson parading the Jules Rimet trophy – along with Liverpool's League Championship, and Everton's FA Cup – around Goodison Park. At the end of the afternoon, Liverpool also had the Shield to take home, thanks to Hunt's first-half winner.

It was another 18 years before the same teams had both their names on the two big domestic trophies. That led to the 1984 Charity Shield, when Bruce Grobbelaar's own goal resulted in Everton's only victory against Liverpool at Wembley.

RIGHT: World Cup winners Roger Hunt and Ray Wilson parade the Jules Rimet trophy around Goodison before champions Liverpool beat FA Cup-winners Everton to win the 1966 Charity Shield for the first time

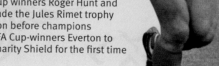

WE SHOULDN'T HAVE BEEN THERE ANYWAY...

Liverpool have twice gone into the Charity Shield as neither League champions or FA Cup holders. In 1971, when Double winners Arsenal declined to take part because of pre-season friendlies, the FA decided the match should be between the FA Cup runners-up and Division Two champions. Liverpool went to Filbert Street, and were beaten 1–0 by Leicester City.

In 2002, with Arsenal having again won the Double, they were paired with Liverpool as Premiership runners-up. This was the first time the trophy was contested under its new name, the Community Shield, and it was Arsenal who won it, thanks – once again – to a single goal.

FA CHARITY/COMMUNITY SHIELD SHARED

Year	Opposition	Result	Venue
1964	West Ham United	2–2	Anfield
1965	Manchester United	2–2	Old Trafford
1977	Manchester United	0–0	Wembley
1986	Everton	1–1	Wembley
1990	Manchester United	1–1	Wembley

FA CHARITY/COMMUNITY SHIELD LOST

Year	Opposition	Result	Venue
1922	Huddersfield	0–1	Old Trafford
1971	Leicester City	0–1	Filbert Street
1983	Manchester United	0–2	Wembley
1984	Everton	0–1	Wembley
1992	Leeds United	3–4	Wembley
2002	Arsenal	0–1	Millennium Stadium

LIVERPOOL'S FIVE BIGGEST DERBY LOSSES		
Date	Result	Venue
9/4/1909	0–5	Goodison Park
3/10/1914	0–5	Anfield
11/1/1902	0–4	Goodison Park
19/9/1964	0–4	Anfield
1/4/1904	2–5	Goodison Park

LIVERPOOL'S FIVE BIGGEST DERBY WINS		
Date	Result	Venue
7/5/1935	6–0	Anfield
25/9/1965	5–0	Anfield
6/11/1982	5–0	Goodison Park
7/10/1922	5–1	Anfield
26/9/1925	5–1	Anfield

RIGHT: Luis Suarez scored the Reds first goal in a 2–1 victory over Everton in the 2012 FA Cup semi-final at Wembley

BELOW: Everton's Peter Reid in action during the goalless 1984 Milk Cup final. Liverpool won the replay 1–0

▼ REDS V BLUES

The most intense and passionate top-flight derby in English football is also currently the longest running, with the big two Merseyside clubs facing each other in every season since 1962.

The fixture itself stretches back to 22 April 1893 when the sides met in a Liverpool Senior Cup tie at Bootle's Hawthorne Road ground. Liverpool won that match 1–0 but were on the wrong end of a 3–0 scoreline in the first League fixture in October

1894 – a match that attracted 44,000 spectators to Goodison Park.

Of the 147 League matches up to the end of the 2012–13 season Liverpool have won 73, drawn 58 and lost 57. The Reds are also ahead in major knockout competitions, winning 12 of the 27 FA and League Cup ties between the two clubs, losing eight and drawing seven. In their three meetings in major domestic finals – the 1984 League Cup and 1986 and 1989 FA Cups – Liverpool have been victorious each time.

▲ SEMI SUCCESS...FINAL FAILURE

Liverpool have won four of the five FA Cup semi-finals in which they've been drawn against their oldest rivals. On the sole occasion Everton won – at Villa Park in 1906 – the Blues went on to lift the trophy. Liverpool won at Maine Road in 1950 and 1977, at Old Trafford in 1971 and at Wembley in 2012. But despite the euphoria after each of those victories, the Reds later lost all four finals.

▼ RUSHIE'S DERBY JOY

Ian Rush is the record goalscorer in Merseyside derbies, finding the net 25 times in 36 appearances. The boyhood Evertonian broke Dixie Dean's long-standing record of 19 goals when he hit a brace in the 1989 FA Cup final. But perhaps his most memorable derby performance came in November 1982 when he was on target four times in the 5–0 League victory at Goodison. Fred Howe is the only other Liverpool player to score four in a derby. His goals came in the 6–0 demolition at Anfield in September 1935.

ABOVE: Rush at the double. For the second time in three years, Ian scored twice against Everton at Wembley

▶ CROSSING THE PARK

Although dozens of players have been on the books of Liverpool and Everton during their careers, just 12 have turned out for both sides in derbies. Of those, only Abel Xavier managed to do it in the same season. The Portuguese defender was in the Everton line-up for the League clash at Goodison in September 2001, but completed his £750,000 move to Liverpool in time to take part in the return fixture at Anfield five months later.

In 1978 Liverpool's David Johnson became the first player to score for both sides in the derby – a feat only matched by Peter Beardsley in 1992, the year after he moved to Everton.

BELOW: From blue to red. David Johnson was the first player to score for both sides in the Merseyside derby. Peter Beardsley is the other

KENNY BREAKS GOODISON CURSE

Of the 14 managers in Liverpool's history, only Kenny Dalglish has managed to win on his first visit to Goodison. In fact, he's done it twice. In 1985, in his opening season as player-boss, Dalglish himself got on the scoresheet after just 20 seconds, setting his team on their way to a 3–2 victory. In October 2011, with him installed in the manager's chair a second time, goals from Luis Suarez and Andy Carroll delivered a 2–0 win at the home of the Blues.

YOU LOOK FAMILIAR...

The record for most derbies in a season was set in 1986–87 when the teams faced each other six times. Apart from the two League fixtures, they met in the Charity Shield, the League Cup Fifth Round, and in two legs of the short-lived Screen Sport Super Cup. Liverpool came out on top in four of the clashes, and managed a draw in the other two. A combined total of 281,356 spectators watched the six games.

THE BLUES AT ANFIELD

Liverpool's 6–0 home League win at Anfield in 1935 still stands as the biggest Merseyside derby victory of all time. The same fixture two years earlier produced the highest scoring derby ever, with the Reds winning 7–4. Between the 1970–71 and 1984–85 seasons Everton failed to win a single match at Anfield, allowing Liverpool to record the longest unbeaten home run in the history of the fixture.

LIVERPOOL'S TOP DERBY MARKSMEN	
Name	Goals
Ian Rush	25
Steven Gerrard	8
Jack Parkinson	8
Harry Chambers	8
Dick Forshaw	7

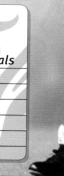

Anfield Legends

Liverpool fans have witnessed many greats over the years. From managers who have delivered silverware to the trophy room, to players who have provided thrills on the pitch. But how many of them can truly be called legends? On what basis can anyone be so described?

Skill alone is not sufficient to warrant the label. Nor is an extensive medal collection. What is crucial is supreme commitment and dedication, an ability to change the direction of the entire club, and an impact that continues to be felt long after a career is over.

No list is definitive, as all supporters have their own opinions and personal favourites. But these legends have not only defined the era in which they served. The stories of their extraordinary achievements and influence will continue to be passed on through the generations.

LEFT: Adoring fans worship at the feet of Bill Shankly after the 1974 FA Cup final

OPPOSITE: Club captain and modern-day legend Steven Gerrard in full flight

Tom Watson

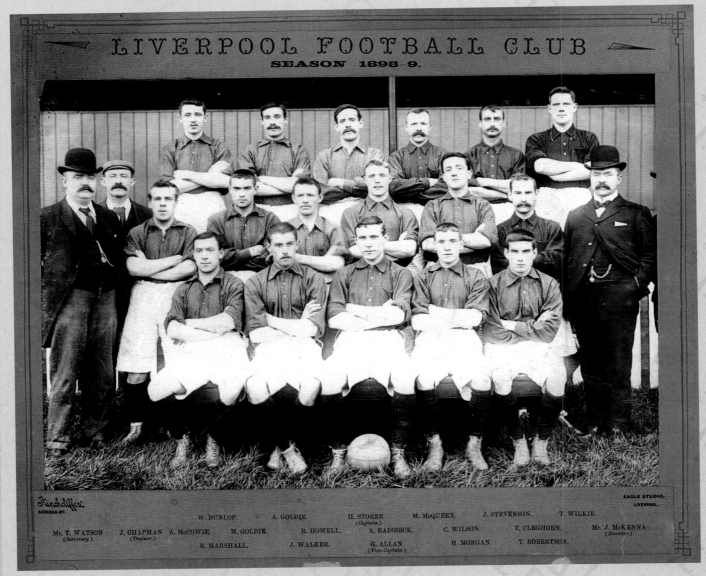

LIVERPOOL FOOTBALL CLUB
SEASON 1898-9.

EAGLE STUDIO,
LIVERPOOL.

W. DUNLOP.   A. GOLDIE.   H. STORER   M. McQUEEN.   J. STEVENSON.   T. WILKIE.
(Captain.)

Mr. T. WATSON   J. CHAPMAN   A. McCOWIE   M. GOLDIE   R. HOWELL,   A. RAISBECK.   C. WILSON.   T. CLEGHORN.   Mr. J. McKENNA
(Secretary.)   (Trainer.)   (Director.)

R. MARSHALL.   J. WALKER.   G. ALLAN   H. MORGAN.   T. ROBERTSON.
(Vice-Captain.)

FROM WEARSIDE TO MERSEYSIDE

Tom Watson was Liverpool's longest-serving manager, the man who changed the club's colours to red, and the first boss to win the League Championship. Club secretary John McKenna recruited the 37-year-old Geordie from Sunderland AFC where he had delivered three Division One titles in four seasons. With his contract coming to an end in the summer of 1896, the North East club were keen for his signature, although not as desperate as McKenna who had just led his own side to promotion and needed a new boss to keep them in the top flight. He offered to double Watson's wages in return for him moving to Merseyside.

TRAINING – THE WATSON WAY

From the moment Watson arrived he set about transforming Liverpool, ushering in a new era of professionalism. He introduced a strict diet and training regime designed to make his players the fittest in the country. Among the rules to be observed were 'strolls' at 7.30am and 7.30pm; regular meals interspersed with vigorous exercise throughout the day; a supper consisting of bread and a glass of beer or claret at 9.30pm, followed by bed half-an-hour later.

He also instructed his team that 'butter, sugar, milk, potatoes and tobacco must be sparingly used'. An interesting order from a man who had once run a tobacconist's shop.

NEW ARRIVALS

Not content with improving the condition of his existing squad, Watson also made a series of big name signings, including Blackpool striker Jack Cox, Sheffield United's England international Raby Howell, plus Scottish central defender Alex Raisbeck for a record fee of £350. In his first season in charge he took the team to their first FA Cup semi-final, then led them to a Division

LEFT: Watson (far left, described as Secretary), with the squad he led to the First Division runners-up spot in 1898–99; two years later, Liverpool FC were champions

OPPOSITE: Liverpool FC's longest serving manager, Watson occupied the Anfield hot seat for 19 years

One runners-up spot two years later. By the end of the 1900–01 season they were top – finishing two points ahead of his old team, Sunderland. To this day, Watson is one of only four men to win the League Championship with two different clubs.

DOWN, UP...AND TOP

Following Watson's first title at Anfield, the Football League introduced new rules capping players' wages at £4 per week, and signing-on fees at £10. It meant that Liverpool, who paid above average salaries, were suddenly unable to attract top talent from other areas of the country. Their fortunes slumped and at the end of the 1903–04 season they were relegated. But Watson the miracle-worker wasn't finished. Twelve months on, his team finished top of Division Two. A year later, they clinched the title again, as he became the first manager to win the Second and First Division Championships in successive seasons. He even came within touching distance of an historic double, but lost to Everton in the FA Cup semi-final at Villa Park.

Following his first crop of signings, Watson had added a second wave, including the great goalkeepers Ned Doig and Sam Hardy, who became England's first choice No. 1. He later added the Scottish international Kenny Campbell, and the young Irishman, and future legend, Elisha Scott. His strikers included Sam Raybould, the first Reds player to hit 30 goals in a season, and Bootle-born Jack Parkinson, whose 219 games yielded an incredible 128 goals.

TRAVELLING MAN

According to one press report, Watson was 'in the habit of taking his holidays abroad ... it is not too much to say that he has had a distinct influence on popularising the game on the continent'. He was keen to introduce his team to foreign lands too, taking them on their first European tour in 1910 and playing a series of matches in Sweden and Denmark. When they returned to Scandinavia in 1914, Liverpool proved to be a big draw, entertaining crowds of up to 16,000. For Watson, the tours were a chance for his players to learn new techniques – and for him to scout new talent. After one match, he made an unsuccessful bid to sign the Gothenburg and Sweden international striker, Erik Borjesson.

FIRST FINAL, LAST MATCH

The 1914 tour came just a fortnight after Watson led Liverpool to their first FA Cup final, which they lost 2–0 to Burnley. It was to be his last highlight as manager. At the end of the following campaign the League programme was suspended due to World War I. On the last day of the season, Liverpool travelled to Oldham where Watson became ill in the Boundary Park dug-out. Twelve days later he died of pneumonia at his home in Priory Road, a stone's throw from the club he had served for almost 19 years.

Tom Watson was undoubtedly Liverpool's first great manager, and his legacy survives to this day. His success meant the club finally emerged from the shadow of their more successful neighbours, Everton. And it gave the board the financial means to expand Anfield and build what would become the most famous terrace in world football: the Kop.

Elisha Scott

SIBLING SCOUT

Belfast-born Elisha Scott was a teenager when his elder brother – and former Everton keeper – Billy, alerted Liverpool to his incredible talent. Reds boss Tom Watson invited him for a trial on 26 August 1912, and signed him from Broadway United five days later. It was a remarkable bit of business. Watson had landed Scott for free, but the youngster showed his potential worth on his debut four months later: within minutes of the final whistle, opponents Newcastle offered £1,000 for his signature.

LIVERPOOL'S NUMBER ONE

It was just as well Liverpool resisted Newcastle's bid, as Scott went on to spend more than two decades on Merseyside, becoming the most popular player Anfield had ever known. Although used as an understudy before the outbreak of war, he became the undisputed first

choice afterwards, keeping his regular place for well over a decade. During that time he won successive League Championship medals in 1922 and 1923, missing only three matches in the two campaigns, and conceding just 61 goals in 83 matches. He also made his debut for Ireland, going on to win 27 caps in an international career lasting 14 years.

BRITAIN'S BEST

By common consent, Scott was far and away the best goalkeeper of his era, attracting rave reviews whenever he played. One newspaper described him as having 'the eye of an eagle, the swift movement of a panther when flinging himself at a shot, and the clutch of a vice when gripping the ball'. Years later, Everton's legendary striker Dixie Dean, who had many epic 'derby-day' battles with Scott, rated him as the best he had seen in his lifetime.

OPPOSITE TOP: Elisha Scott had "the clutch of a vice when gripping the ball"

OPPOSITE BELOW: Trademark clothing. Scott in roll-neck jersey and long-johns

RIGHT: Scott, pictured near the end of his 21-year Liverpool career

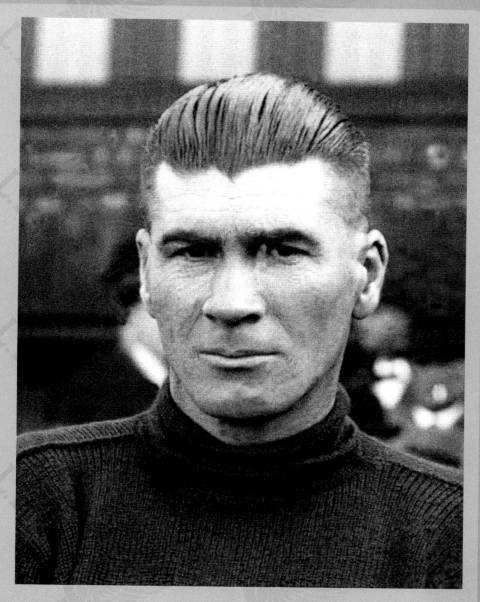

He was also obsessive about fitness. Team-mates described how he practised longer, and trained harder than all of them. When sessions were over he would spend hours throwing the ball against a wall to catch it on the rebound. Rather than take the tram, he would then walk the three miles from Anfield to the Mersey Ferry terminal to catch the boat back to his home in New Brighton.

MIND YOUR LANGUAGE!

A famous set of photos, taken in the late 1920s, show Scott kitted out in roll-neck jersey, long-johns, socks and knee pads. This trademark dress was as familiar to Liverpudlians as his industrial-strength language which, according to some reports, could be heard echoing around the ground on match days. No one was safe from the abuse, especially his own defenders. It entertained the crowd but so disgusted Reds centre-back – and future Presbyterian minister – Jimmy Jackson that he once remarked to an opponent: 'I shall never play in front of that man again!'

THE LONG GOODBYE

During the early 1930s, an ageing Scott began to struggle for a regular first-team place, and was transfer-listed. Liverpool were prepared to accept an audacious £250 bid from Everton, and for a short time during the 1933–34 League campaign it looked like Elisha and his old adversary Dixie Dean would become team-mates. Only a concerted effort by Reds' supporters, who bombarded the *Liverpool Echo* with protest letters, forced the Anfield board to reconsider. But it was clear that Scott's time was coming to an end. Soon afterwards he decided to

leave anyway, lured by the offer of a player-manager role with Belfast Celtic. After the final home game of the 1933–34 season, he was allowed to address the Anfield crowd from the director's box. For once the hard-man mask slipped as he ended an emotional speech with the words: 'Last but not least, my friends on the Kop. I cannot thank them sufficiently. They have inspired me. God bless you all.'

FROM PLAYER TO BOSS

After returning to Northern Ireland, Scott played on until the age of 42. He then settled in to the manager's role full-time, gaining a reputation as a fierce disciplinarian and master tactician. He guided Belfast Celtic to 10 Irish League titles and six Irish

Cups, and would surely have won even more silverware had the club not been forced to withdraw from the league in 1949 due to serious sectarian problems. He was offered other managerial posts, but after such a long and illustrious career, he decided the time was right to retire. Elisha died in 1959 following a series of strokes.

HOLDING ON TO HIS RECORD

The passage of time has meant that many of the records set by Scott have been eclipsed. In terms of clean sheets, he now stands behind Ray Clemence, Bruce Grobbelaar and Jose Reina. But to this day, no one can match his longevity as a player. By the time he left, he'd been with Liverpool for 21 years and 52 days.

Billy Liddell

THE GREATEST RED

William Beveridge Liddell arrived at Anfield as a 16-year-old and played his last game at the age of 39. In the intervening years he shattered Liverpool's appearances and goals records and – for the generation lucky enough to watch – established himself as the finest player in LFC's history. Ian Callaghan, who's seen a few come and go in his time, is in no doubt: 'In my opinion, Liddell, Keegan and Dalglish were the club's best players ever. But I would put Billy ahead of the other two as being the greatest.' One League Championship medal and an FA Cup runners-up medal were all he had to show at the end of his club career. But the lack of awards was in stark contrast to the impact Billy Liddell had on Liverpool.

LATE STARTER

The outbreak of World War II, just a year after Liddell moved down from his native Scotland, delayed the start of his Football League career until 1946. He did manage to play in 152 of Liverpool's wartime games, but even these were interrupted by RAF service. Once he was de-mobbed he walked straight into the post-war side, making 35 appearances on the left wing and playing a huge part in securing the First Division title. His speed and skill tormented defences, mesmerised crowds and had reporters scratching their heads to come up with new superlatives. Already an established Scottish international, Liddell was selected to represent Great Britain in a match against the Rest of Europe at the end of the season.

MAN FOR ALL SEASONS

Although Liverpool went into decline after their Championship success, Liddell was remarkably consistent. He was top scorer in four of their last five seasons in the top flight, and three during their time in Division Two. He became renowned for his cannonball shot, famously ripping the net in one game against Tottenham at White Hart Lane, and fracturing the arm of Nottingham Forest keeper Harry Nicholson, who had foolishly tried to stop one of his free kicks. His power wasn't limited to his feet. When Portsmouth visited Anfield in 1948, he opened the scoring with a header – from outside the penalty area. But that was nothing compared to the match six years later when he headed with such force that the ball actually burst. Despite his phenomenal strength, Liddell was the cleanest player in the game. In 534 appearances he never received a single caution.

'LIDDELLPOOL'

Following relegation in 1954 the club relied on Liddell more than ever. He played in all four forward positions, helped in midfield and even filled in as an emergency full-back. The Reds became such a one-man team that newspapers routinely referred to them as 'Liddellpool'. He was still in the form of his life, good enough to be selected for the elite Great Britain XI for a second time in 1955. Yet, in a show of loyalty that would mystify modern supporters, he remained staunchly committed to the club that gave him his first chance. He wasn't short of offers, either from home or abroad. He even turned down a lucrative bid from the South American side Santa Fe, based in the Colombian capital Bogota. When they made a second attempt to lure him away he was adamant: 'All my interests are here at Anfield and I should hate to leave.'

RED JERSEY, WHITE COLLAR

Throughout his playing career Liddell held down a nine-to-five job as an accountant, working in a city centre office, and only joining his team-mates for training twice a week. For a footballer he was, even in those days, a breed apart: a non-drinking, non-smoking Methodist lay-preacher, who undertook tireless charity work and gave up his time to work as a hospital radio DJ for free. He also served as a magistrate for four years and, once

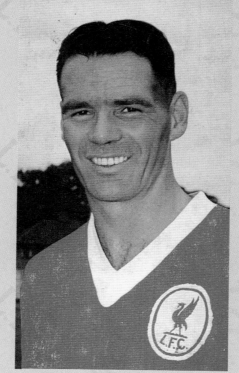

his playing days were over, became Bursar at the University of Liverpool.

BREAKING RECORDS TO THE END

Liddell hit the last of his 228 goals in a home match against Stoke in March 1960. He was 38 years and 55 days, and remains the oldest player to score for the club. Although he played his final competitive game five months later, there was one more appearance still to come. In September that year, the Anfield board granted him a testimonial in which the Reds took on an International XI. Some of the names in that opposition line-up reveal the esteem in which Liddell was held throughout the football world: Bert Trautmann, Don Revie, Stanley Matthews, Nat Lofthouse, Tom Finney. But perhaps the biggest tribute was the 39,000 crowd – 10,000 more than the average Anfield League gate that same season.

Bill Shankly

THE MAN WHO CHANGED EVERYTHING

Liverpool was a byword for underachievement in the 1950s. The once successful club still had a huge following, but languished in the Second Division, never quite good enough to clamber back to the top flight or challenge for honours. But at the end of that decade a 46-year-old Scot arrived to wake the sleeping giant. He was Bill Shankly: the most charismatic manager in the history of Liverpool FC.

PLANNING FOR PROMOTION

Shankly inherited a squad full of ageing and average players. He got rid of 24 of them in his first year, holding on to promising youngsters like Roger Hunt and Ian Callaghan, and recruiting new players such as centre-half Ron Yeats and midfielder Gordon Milne. He also persuaded the board to spend a record £37,500 on the fiery Motherwell striker Ian St. John.

The manager introduced a high-intensity training regime designed to develop the five attributes he considered essential in every top player: skill, speed, strength, stamina and flexibility. The new players responded perfectly, storming to the Second Division Championship in the 1961–62 season. Eight years after relegation, Liverpool were back where they belonged.

SHANKLY AND THE KOP

From the outset, Shankly had an incredible bond with the club's supporters, inspiring a devotion unrivalled in the game. He reminded them that he used to turn out in front of the Kop as a player with Preston North End, and had always regarded those who stood there as 'the best fans in the world'. He called on the crowd to make as much noise as possible during games, encouraged the development of singing on the terraces, and started the tradition of playing 'You'll Never Walk Alone' before kick-off.

The supporters responded, forging Anfield's reputation as the loudest, most atmospheric ground in the land. Shankly was their hero, and they lapped up every one of his famous quotes designed to build their own club up, and bring the opposition down. But the admiration was mutual. In later years he revealed that his obsession with establishing Liverpool as the greatest club in the land stemmed from a burning desire 'to make the people happy'.

THE TITLES – AND THE CUP
In 1964, Shankly led Liverpool to their first League title in 17 years, a triumph that paved the way for the club's first forays into Europe. Just two seasons later they were Champions again. In between those successes came what he later described as his 'greatest day': the 1965 FA Cup final against Leeds. Liverpool had not won the trophy in their 73-year history and, for many supporters, lifting the Cup had become an obsession.

Shankly's team brought their agonising wait to an end with a 2–1 win at Wembley, thanks to goals from Hunt and St. John. It led to the first of many unforgettable homecomings and victory parades through the streets of the city for Shankly and his men.

PARADISE LOST – AND REGAINED
The team that swept all before them in the mid-sixties went into decline as the decade ended, and Shankly began the process of dismantling and rebuilding. In the 1971–72 season, his new side, including fresh faces like Ray Clemence, Steve Heighway, Kevin Keegan and John Toshack, finished as First Division runners-up. Just a year later they went one better, winning the Championship, as well as the UEFA Cup – Liverpool's first European trophy. Shankly was named Manager of the Year after landing the club's first ever double, but the era of the club's dominance was only beginning. At the end of the following season he led his team back to Wembley, where Keegan inspired them to a 3–0 win over Newcastle, and their second FA Cup.

RESIGNATION AND RETIREMENT
In July 1974 Shankly told Liverpool he wanted to quit – a decision the club accepted with 'extreme reluctance'. Supporters were devastated, and he himself likened his resignation to 'walking to the electric chair'. He blamed his decision on 'tiredness', although it was plain that he regretted it soon afterwards. Despite working as an advisor to other football clubs, he desperately missed full-time involvement in the game to which he had devoted his life.

Shankly's one great regret as a manager was not winning the European Cup. He did get to see the team lift the trophy three times. But then, on 29 September 1981, he died in hospital following a heart attack. The football world mourned the passing of one of its most outstanding managers, and its greatest-ever character. His ashes were later spread around his beloved Anfield.

OPPOSITE TOP: Shanks leads out the team for the 1971 FA Cup final against Arsenal

OPPOSITE LEFT: Bill Shankly after winning his third First Division title in 1973

TOP: Shanks in familiar pose, accepting the plaudits from his fans on the terraces

ABOVE: Dream Team: Bill Shankly with his long-term assistant, Bob Paisley (left)

SHANKLY'S MAJOR HONOURS
1961–62: Second Division Championship
1963–64: League Championship
1964–65: FA Cup
1965–66: League Championship
1972–73: League Championship, UEFA Cup
1973–74: FA Cup

Roger Hunt

GOALS GALORE

Roger Hunt found the net on his 1959 debut, and carried on scoring for the next decade. His League record of 245 goals – scored in 404 matches – remains intact to this day. As does his incredible tally of 41 goals in as many games during the 1961–62 campaign. Hunt topped the club's scoring charts for nine seasons – a feat only equalled by Ian Rush. Throughout his time at Anfield his instincts in front of goal were without parallel. Of the 286 he scored in all competitions, only one of them came from the penalty spot.

EARLY DAYS

Hunt was signed from the non-League side Stockton Heath and broke into Liverpool's first team within a year. Three months after his debut appearance, Bill Shankly arrived and embarked on a mass clear-out of the players he inherited. As one of the few survivors, Hunt was desperate to return the new manager's faith. 'I knew perfectly well that I wasn't an out-and-out natural, the sort who can make a ball talk, so it was down to me to compensate for it in other ways,' he later recalled. 'I made up

my mind that if I didn't succeed at Anfield, it wouldn't be for the lack of determination. I threw myself into training, ran and tackled for everything and practised my ball skills at every opportunity.'

Hunt's determination paid off, as he delivered countless match-winning performances. His form in the 1961–62 season, when he scored an unprecedented five League hat-tricks, was largely responsible for the team's promotion from Division Two. Once in the top flight, he opened the country's elite defences with equal ease. In both 1964 and 1966, when Liverpool won the Championship, Hunt hit 33 goals – more than a third of the team's totals for each season.

ROGER'S RECORD

Competition	Games	Goals
League	404	245
FA Cup	44	18
League Cup	10	5
Europe	31	17
Charity Shield	1	1
All Comps	492	286

HUNT FOR THE CUP

The road to Liverpool's 1965 FA Cup triumph started at West Brom where Hunt set them on their way to a Third Round victory. Four months later the team faced Leeds at Wembley – where he became the first LFC player to score in an FA Cup final. Although his headed goal in extra time was subsequently cancelled out, he still ended up on the winning side thanks to Ian St. John's dramatic late winner. Hunt went on to score 18 FA Cup goals during his Liverpool career – a record that stood for nearly two decades.

LIVERPOOL'S BOY OF '66

The prolific form shown at club level earned Hunt an England call-up while Liverpool were still in the Second Division. His international debut came in April 1962 when he scored in a 3–1 Wembley win against Austria, and he was impressive enough to be called up for that year's World Cup finals. He never made an appearance at the tournament in Chile, but four years later it was a different matter.

Hunt scored three times as England made their way to the final, and was in the line-up the day they beat West Germany.

Liverpool's first World Cup winner faced hostility from many southern fans and journalists who regarded him as a 'workhorse' and resented his inclusion in the side ahead of the 'showman' Jimmy Greaves. But no England manager could ignore Hunt's formidable scoring record for his country. As he himself reminded his critics some years later: 'I don't think I've done too badly…I have made more international appearances than any other Liverpool player. During my 34 matches I have scored 18 goals and only finished on the losing side twice.'

KNIGHT OF THE KOP

Hunt's Liverpool career came to an end in December 1969, finishing much as it had started. In one of his final appearances at Anfield he came off the bench to score two goals in the last 10 minutes. But there was

OPPOSITE TOP: Roger Hunt in action in a 1–1 draw with Burnley on Boxing Day, 1968

OPPOSITE LEFT: Roger during 1968–69 season – which he finished as Liverpool's top scorer for the ninth time

BELOW: Roger and out: Hunt in his final season for Liverpool, facing Spurs at White Hart Lane

no denying that his best days were behind him, and the club were willing to let him move to Bolton where he could continue to enjoy first-team football until his retirement in 1972. In that same year, nearly 56,000 fans turned out for his Anfield testimonial, all eager to give personal thanks to the man they referred to as 'Sir' Roger. For many who watched Liverpool in the sixties, Hunt is still their idol. For those who played alongside him, he remains the ultimate predator in front of goal: 'Fernando Torres is the nearest thing I have ever seen to him,' said former captain, Tommy Smith. 'When I pick my greatest ever Liverpool team then Roger Hunt is the first forward I put in.'

Kevin Keegan

WHAT A STEAL!

There were some amazingly talented players in Liverpool's early-seventies side: from the older stalwarts like Smith, Hughes and Callaghan, to hungry youngsters such as Clemence, Heighway and Toshack. But the man who ignited Bill Shankly's second revolution was a short, muscular 20-year-old from Yorkshire. Kevin Keegan electrified Liverpool from the day he made his debut in 1971 to the night they won their first European Cup in 1977. For six years he was the most exciting player in Britain. In later seasons he would be voted the best footballer in Europe. And he cost the Reds just £33,000. No wonder Shankly described the deal as 'not just robbery...but robbery with violence.'

DUSTBIN DAYS

Liverpool's future talisman began his football career in the unpromising amateur surroundings of the Pegler's Brass Works team in Doncaster. After being turned down by Coventry he went for a trial at Scunthorpe United and was offered professional terms at the age of 17.

It was Shankly's friend Andy Beattie who alerted Liverpool to a hidden gem, buried away in England's lowest league division. When Keegan was invited to Anfield to discuss a contract offer the meeting was delayed, and he had to sit on a dustbin in the Main Stand car park while he waited. Later that afternoon he became a Liverpool player, and began an intense father-and-son-like relationship with his new boss. 'Kevin was one of the most honest boys of all time,' said Shankly. 'His father had a mining background like me,

KEEGAN'S COLLECTION

With Liverpool: 3 League Championships, 1 European Cup, 2 UEFA Cups, 1 FA Cup

With Hamburg: 2 Bundesligas

63 England Caps

Footballer of the Year, 1976

Ballon D'Or: 1978, 1979

so we understood each other. Kevin was a born winner – all action and all energy.'

A STAR IS BORN

Keegan caused havoc on his debut against Nottingham Forest, scoring after 12 minutes and winning a penalty just three minutes later. It was clear from that first home game of the 1971–72 season that Liverpool had discovered a phenomenal talent. Keegan simply never stopped running. He was fearless, possessed blistering pace, was strong in the tackle, could dribble, shoot with both feet, and out-jump defenders who towered above him. As the campaign wore on he forged a close understanding with Toshack, and their goals powered the Reds to a Championship runners-up spot. But it was in the following season – when the relationship became almost telepathic – that Liverpool swept all before them to clinch their first title in seven years.

THE BIG STAGE

The best players perform in big games – and no one rose to the occasion like Keegan. He scored Liverpool's first ever goals in a European final, hitting the target twice in the first leg UEFA Cup victory over Borussia Moenchengladbach in 1973. Three years later he popped up with the equaliser in the UEFA Cup final second leg at FC Bruges, securing the trophy for a second time. But he reserved his greatest performances for two other finals. The first was at Wembley in 1974 when he ran Newcastle ragged and scored twice in the 3–0 FA Cup win. The second was in Rome in 1977: his last ever-appearance in a Liverpool shirt.

THE SWANSONG SEASON

By the mid-seventies Keegan had become football's first true modern-day superstar. He was an England regular who had transcended his sport to become a household name. But, after five years of success at home and abroad with Liverpool, he craved a new challenge. Shortly after winning his second League Championship medal in 1976, he announced his intention to spend just one more season at Anfield.

After the initial shock subsided, some voiced fears that he was no longer fully committed to the Liverpool cause. But they were wrong. He went on to play 57 games in a season that brought yet another League title, and appearances in both the FA and European Cup finals. The Wembley match against Manchester United ended in disappointment. But just four days later Keegan put on the performance of his life as Liverpool beat Borussia Moenchengladbach 3–1 at Rome's Olympic Stadium. For once he wasn't on the scoresheet, but his endless raids past the Germans' defence caused them to resort to desperate measures. After one particularly blatant foul, Liverpool were awarded a penalty, duly converted by Phil Neal.

LIFE AFTER LIVERPOOL

Keegan joined the German side SV Hamburg in the summer of 1977, later winning two Bundesliga titles and twice being voted European Footballer of the Year. He went on to play for Southampton and Newcastle, a club he later managed, along with Fulham and Manchester City. Between 1999 and 2000 he served as England manager – the only former Liverpool player to hold the post.

OPPOSITE TOP: Despite his size, many of Keegan's 100 Liverpool goals came from headers

OPPOSITE LEFT: Keegan runs onto the Anfield pitch during the 1974–75 season

BELOW: German international Berti Vogts hauls down Keegan to concede a penalty during the 1977 European Cup final

Bob Paisley

THE RELUCTANT HERO

Bob Paisley was as surprised as anyone when Bill Shankly announced his resignation in July 1974. He was even more shocked to be offered the manager's position himself. Paisley, who had been on the club's staff since retiring as a player two decades earlier, initially refused, and even pleaded with Shankly to change his mind and come back. But after pressure from the LFC board he reluctantly accepted the job in time for the 1974–75 season. It's a good thing they were so determined to persuade him. Paisley turned out to be the most successful manager in Liverpool's history.

DOMESTIC DOMINANCE

In Paisley's nine years in charge Liverpool dominated the domestic game like no other club had done before. He followed up his trophy-less first season with a League and UEFA Cup double in 1976, and further titles in 1977, 1979, 1980, 1982 and 1983. After losing a League Cup final in 1978, he finally delivered the trophy for the first time in 1981, then retained it for two years running. His success at home led to annual trips to Wembley for the Charity Shield, which he ended up winning five times.

ROME, LONDON AND PARIS

Paisley achieved immortality as a result of his triumphs with the Reds abroad. No other manager in the world can match his achievement of winning the European Cup three times. He first enjoyed success on the continent with the 1976 UEFA Cup victory over FC Bruges. But that two-legged affair turned out to be a mere taster. A year later he guided the team to the ultimate prize in Rome with a 3–1 win against Borussia Moenchengladbach. As Liverpool's players, and their thousands of ecstatic travelling fans, geared up for an epic night of celebrations, Paisley refused all offers of alcohol, telling anyone who asked: 'I just want to savour every moment.'

After becoming the first Englishman ever to lead a team to European Cup success, Paisley then retained it at Wembley the following year. He completed the hat-trick in Paris in 1981 as the Reds beat Real Madrid. His incredible record at home and overseas may never have brought him the knighthood he so richly deserved, but his achievements were recognised by his fellow professionals. Between 1976 and 1983 he was voted Manager of the Year six times.

PLAYER, COACH AND BACK-ROOM BOY

Long before he was manager, Paisley was a highly successful player, noted for his toughness. Writing about Liverpool's 1946–47 Championship side, one reporter noted: 'This North East young man has little height, two stout limbs, a heart of gold and a tackle that is riotous. He has tenacity written all over his face.' Paisley was a regular in the side until Liverpool's relegation in 1954. His one great disappointment was being left out of the 1950 FA Cup final – a decision that almost caused him to leave. He later served as physio, reserve team manager, coach, and assistant to Bill Shankly. But he was most proud of his time as first-team trainer when he developed an expert knowledge of how to instil fitness, diagnose injuries and supervise their treatment.

PAISLEY'S PLAYERS

Some of Liverpool's greatest ever players made their debuts during Paisley's reign. Among his wisest buys were Kenny Dalglish, Graeme Souness, Alan Hansen, Terry McDermott, Steve Nicol, Ian Rush and Mark Lawrenson. Youngsters brought through the ranks included Jimmy Case, David Fairclough and Sammy Lee. Paisley had a knack of getting the absolute best out of players, even if it meant changing their traditional roles in the team. Ray Kennedy was signed as an out-and-out striker, but his manager converted him into one of the finest midfielders Anfield has ever seen.

BOB'S LEGACY

When Paisley handed over to Joe Fagan in 1983 he was by far the most successful manager in English football history. Who knows how many more trophies he would have won had he not delayed his managerial career until the age of 56? What is beyond doubt is the huge level of respect and admiration his record still commands. At Anfield – where the Paisley Gateway stands in his honour – he will always be remembered as the man who built on the foundations laid by Bill Shankly, and brought even greater success to the club he served for 44 years.

OPPOSITE TOP: A very good year: Bob Paisley with his trophy haul and managerial awards at the end of the 1980–81 season

OPPOSITE BOTTOM: Training days: Paisley tends to an injured Phil Boersma at Elland Road

BELOW: Bob and friends, with the European Cup and League Championship trophy

PAISLEY'S POTS

1975–76:	League Championship, UEFA Cup
1976–77:	League Championship, European Cup, European Super Cup
1977–78:	European Cup
1978–79:	League Championship
1979–80:	League Championship
1980–81:	European Cup, League Cup
1981–82:	League Championship, League Cup
1982–83:	League Championship, League Cup

Kenny Dalglish

A MAN APART

Dalglish played during the most successful period in the club's history, and was the ultimate star in a team of world-beaters. According to Paisley: 'Of all the players I have played alongside, managed and coached in more than 40 years at Anfield, he is the most talented.' His playing career alone would qualify him as an all-time club legend, but two further factors set Dalglish apart from all others. Firstly, his subsequent spells as manager, which yielded yet more silverware. Even more importantly, his heroic efforts to unify the club and its supporters following the devastating tragedy of Hillsborough.

CREATOR AND FINISHER

Dalglish's £440,000 transfer from Celtic was a record deal between British clubs. But he began repaying the fee immediately, hitting six goals in his first seven League games. By the time he hung up his boots he'd found the net 172 times – but those goals are only half the story. His ability to hold up play, allied with his incredible vision, touch and timing, made him 'the creator supreme'. Record goalscorer Ian Rush later acknowledged the debt he owed to his brilliant partner: 'I just made the runs, knowing the ball would come to me.' Under Paisley, Dalglish won two European Cups, three League Championships and three League Cups. In Joe Fagan's first season he helped land an historic League, European Cup and League Cup treble.

IN THE HOT SEAT

After succeeding Fagan, Dalglish guided Liverpool to a League and FA Cup double in his first season – a

DAWN OF A NEW ERA

Kevin Keegan's departure after the 1977 European Cup triumph left a gap at Liverpool that few thought could be filled. But Bob Paisley knew differently. In the immediate aftermath of the Rome final, he told reporters he was looking forward to the future with relish: 'Obviously we'll miss Kevin but we have plans for a replacement who could bring a whole new dimension to our play.' That replacement turned out to be Kenny Dalglish who, just 12 months later, scored the goal that delivered Paisley's second European Cup.

KENNY'S MEDAL CABINET

With Celtic: 4 Scottish Championships, 3 Scottish Cups, 1 Scottish League Cup

With Liverpool (as player): 6 League Championships, 3 European Cups, 2 FA Cups, 4 League Cups, 1 European Super Cup, 3 Manager of the Year Awards, 2 Footballer of the Year Awards, 1 PFA Player of the Year Award

With Liverpool (as manager): 3 League Championships, 2 FA Cups, 1 League Cup

With Blackburn Rovers: 1 Premier League Championship, 1 Manager of the Year Award

With Scotland: 102 caps

unique feat for a player-boss, and one that brought him the first of four Manager of the Year awards. As his own appearances became less frequent, he recruited new talent like John Barnes, Peter Beardsley, Ray Houghton and John Aldridge, creating one of the most exciting front-lines in the history of the English game. Sadly, although his teams won three League titles and two FA Cups, the ban imposed after the Heysel disaster meant they were never able to compete in Europe. However, it was another tragedy that cast the greatest shadow over Dalglish's managerial reign.

HILLSBOROUGH AND AFTER

After witnessing the Hillsborough disaster unfold, Dalglish vowed to do all he could for the families of the dead. He visited the injured in hospital, including a teenage boy in a coma, who later died. He consoled the bereaved and ensured the club was represented at every funeral. He and wife Marina went to countless services themselves, even attending four in a single day.

Hillsborough took its toll on Dalglish. Almost two years later, he told the board he felt unable to carry on as Liverpool manager.

SECOND COMING

By October 1991, a recovered Dalglish made a managerial comeback with Blackburn Rovers, who he led to the Premiership title four years later. There were further spells at Newcastle and Celtic before he bowed out of the game to focus on media work.

Dalglish returned to Liverpool in 1991 to head the Youth Academy and assume an ambassadorial role. In January 2011 the board asked him to succeed Roy Hodgson on a temporary basis, although the transformation in the team's performances – and supporters' spirits – meant he was soon offered the role permanently. In the event, his only full season in charge was 2011–12, when the team finished a disappointing eighth in the Premier League.

But success in the League Cup brought the club its first silverware in six years. It also made Dalglish the only Liverpool manager to win trophies in three different decades.

OPPOSITE TOP: Dalglish celebrates his title-clinching winner at Stamford Bridge in May 1986

OPPOSITE BOTTOM: Kenny Dalglish with his second Footballer of the Year award in 1983

BELOW: Return to the dugout: Dalglish gives instructions to Steven Gerrard during his second spell as Liverpool FC manager

Alan Hansen

TRIAL AND ERROR

Alan Hansen was a brilliant all-round sportsman who had the chance to represent his country at basketball, volleyball, squash and golf. He also could have played for Liverpool sooner than he did – if he hadn't failed a trial at the age of 16. Back then the young Scot was skinny, un-coordinated, and unable to 'meet the requirements of LFC'. But six years later he was back, and forcing his way into the first team. By the time he retired he was one of the most decorated players in the club's history.

TREBLE SCOTCH

Hansen was one of three Scots signed by Bob Paisley within a 12 month period, all of whom went on to become pivotal figures in Liverpool's most successful era. Although younger than both Graeme Souness and Kenny Dalglish, he displayed a maturity beyond his years, exuding cool while under pressure in defence,

and launching countless attacks with his forward surges.

The £100,000 capture from Partick Thistle made his debut in September 1977, and completed his first Anfield campaign by earning a place in the 1978 European Cup final line-up as a full-back. But during the following season he edged out the long-serving Emlyn Hughes to make one of the two centre-back berths his own. The impact was immediate. With Hansen at the heart of the defence for much of the 1978–79 season, Liverpool conceded only 16 goals.

BUILDING FROM THE BACK

Paisley once complained that Hansen gave him 'more heart attacks than any other player'. The reason? His penchant for dribbling his way out of defence rather than opting for the long clearance. Such was his patience and composure on the ball that some critics labelled him 'the Scottish Beckenbauer' – perhaps the classiest

HANSEN BUNCH

8	League Championships
3	European Cups
2	FA Cups
4	League Cups
26	Scotland caps

central defender the game has ever known.

Hansen was long legged, skilful and deceptively fast. His mid-eighties partnership with master-of-the-tackle Mark Lawrenson is widely regarded as the most effective Liverpool defensive pairing ever. Both were at the heart of the side that won an unprecedented League, European Cup and League Cup treble in 1983–84 – with Hansen playing in all 67 games.

CAPTAIN'S DOUBLE

When Dalglish took over as player-manager in 1985 one of his first acts was to hand the captaincy to his great friend and countryman. Hansen rose to the challenge, hitting the form of his life and appearing in 49 of the 50 League and FA Cup games that season. At the end of the campaign, he lifted the Cup at Wembley, celebrating not only victory over Everton, but the club's historic double.

Hansen was never famed for his tackling abilities – preferring to use his superb anticipation and vision to cut off supply lines to opposing strikers – but the strain of playing so many games over such a long period was beginning to take its toll. Towards the end of the double-winning season he was unable to take to the pitch without the aid of painkilling injections to his knees.

THE SWANSONG SEASONS

After helping Dalglish put together the 'great entertainers' who swept all before them in the 1987–88 season, Hansen's knee problems worsened. The following year he was restricted to just eight appearances as Gary Gillespie took his place and Ronnie Whelan assumed the captaincy. He was recalled for the ill-fated 1989 FA Cup semi-final at Hillsborough, and for the Wembley final against Everton, but it was Whelan who was given the honour of lifting the trophy.

He was able to give the club one more season – the 1989–90 campaign in which they clinched their 18th League title. But shortly afterwards, following his 620th appearance, he decided to bow out on medical advice.

CLUB AND COUNTRY

Given Hansen's imperious form at Europe's top club side, it's incredible that he only won 26 Scottish caps. Even more astonishing was the reason given by successive national coaches: that they didn't want to disrupt the successful central defensive partnership of Willie Miller and Alex McLeish. Hansen did appear at the 1982 World Cup finals in Spain, but Scotland boss Alex Ferguson dropped him from the 1986 squad blaming his reluctance to play in international friendlies in the run up to the tournament. A wise choice on the player's part, as Liverpool were chasing the double at the time.

TELLING IT LIKE IT IS...

Following his retirement, many hoped that Hansen would join the Anfield coaching staff and prepare for future management. But he chose to quit the game completely and forge a new career in TV. Since joining the BBC's *Match of the Day* team in the early 1990s he's proved to be the most accomplished of pundits, never afraid to offer a strong opinion. But although he may be impartial in the studio, he's a committed Red once the cameras are off.

OPPOSITE TOP: Captain at the double: Alan Hansen leads the 1986 FA Cup final lap of honour, just a week after lifting the League Championship

OPPOSITE LEFT: Hansen celebrates one of his 14 goals for the club

ABOVE: Sign of the times: Hansen with autograph hunters before the final League match of the title-winning 1987–88 season

Ian Rush

ULTIMATE PREDATOR

Ian Rush is Liverpool's all-time top scorer and one of the greatest strikers in the history of the game. In his two spells at Anfield he was on target 346 times in 660 appearances. He has more goals in the FA Cup than any other player of the 20th century, and has scored more in finals than anyone since the competition began. He was the first player to collect five League Cup winner's medals and is the tournament's joint leading marksman. He's also scored more goals for his country than any other Welshman.

RUSHIE'S GOALS

Competition	Games	Goals
League	469	229
FA Cup	61	39
League Cup	78	48
Europe	38	20
Charity Shield	7	3
Screen Sport Super Cup	4	7
Other	3	0
All Comps	660	346

SLOW STARTER, DEADLY FINISHER

Bob Paisley paid £300,000 to bring the 18-year-old Rush from Chester to Liverpool – then a record fee for a teenager. But the striker suffered an unhappy start to his Anfield career, starting just nine games in the 1980–81 season and failing to score in any of them. When he found himself back in the reserves at the start of the following campaign he demanded an explanation from Paisley. The response was blunt: 'You don't score enough goals, so you're not worth your place.' Rush considered leaving but then decided to fight for his place and prove his manager wrong. After breaking his duck in a European Cup tie against Oulun Palloseura, the scoring instinct he'd shown at Chester came back to life. By the end of the season he had 30 goals to his name and had replaced David Johnson as the first-choice centre-forward.

1983–84: A VINTAGE SEASON

Rush broke the 30-goal barrier in five different campaigns and hit the 40-mark twice. His partnership with Kenny Dalglish proved lethal; the former supplying the passes, the latter making the runs into the box. Rush was fast and agile, strong in the air, and packed a powerful shot with either foot. He hit his most devastating form in the 1983–84 treble winning season, when he struck 32 goals in the League – including five in one match against Luton – and 15 more in domestic and European knockout competitions. Along with his team medals he was named Footballer of the Year and PFA Player of the Year, and was awarded the European Golden Boot.

THE LOSING SIDE AT LAST

For his first six years at Anfield Rush held one of the club's most unusual records: in the 145 games in which he scored, Liverpool were never beaten. The record became so well-known that opposing teams' heads dropped as soon as he got off the mark. When he grabbed the equaliser in the 1986

FA Cup final a number of Everton players said they knew they were going to lose. But all good things come to an end, and for Rush and Liverpool, it happened at another Wembley final – the 1987 League Cup against Arsenal. Rush put the Reds in front, but the Gunners hit back twice to lift the trophy.

THE ITALIAN JOB

The post-Heysel European ban hit Liverpool's finances hard and they were soon forced to part with their most valuable asset. The club had paid £300,000 for Rush but, seven years on, Juventus were offering more than 10 times that amount for his services. He moved to Turin at the start of the 1987–88 season and went on to score 14 goals – including four in one game. But injuries and problems adapting to Italian culture meant he never fully replicated the form he showed in England. Within a year Juve indicated a willingness to sell him back to Liverpool for £500,000 less than they had spent. Rush jumped at the chance, and everyone at Anfield welcomed him back with open arms.

NORMAL SERVICE RESUMED

Rush's second Liverpool stint began in the 1988–89 season, at the end of which he scored twice against Everton in a 3–2 FA Cup final victory. The following season he was on target 18 times in the League as Liverpool clinched their 18th Championship. Rush surpassed Roger Hunt's scoring record with a goal at Old Trafford in October 1992 – the same year in which he scored against Sunderland at Wembley, taking his tally in FA Cup finals to five. His last goal for Liverpool was in a 2–2 home draw with Manchester City in May 1996. He then joined Leeds United, and had spells with Newcastle, Wrexham and the Australian side Sydney Olympic, before finally retiring.

OPPOSITE TOP: Ian Rush during the 1983–84 campaign – his most productive season in front of goal

OPPOSITE LEFT: Rush in action following his return from Juventus

TOP: Europe's deadliest striker, Rush receives the Golden Boot award in 1984

LEFT: Wembley winner: In 1992, Rush became the first player to score five goals in FA Cup finals

John Barnes

WORLD BEATER

John Barnes attributed his awesome speed, suppleness and agility to a childhood spent in Jamaica. All three were evident when he represented his adopted country, England, at the Maracana Stadium in 1984. His stunning display against the Brazilian world champions – topped by a goal at the end of a mesmerising run – alerted every club in Europe to his astonishing ability. But when he decided to leave Watford three years later, it was Liverpool who won the race for his signature.

BEST OF THE BEST

It was Alan Hansen who convinced boss Kenny Dalglish to sign the 23-year-old, complaining that the team who finished the 1986–87 season was 'the most limited' he had ever played in. Barnes' arrival – along with that of Peter Beardsley, Ray Houghton and John Aldridge –

changed all that. The new side served up the most entertaining brand of football the English game had ever seen. They started with a 29-match unbeaten run, finished with 87 goals, won the Championship with nine points to spare and narrowly missed out on a second double due to a shock defeat in the FA Cup final against Wimbledon.

And it was Barnes who was at the heart of it all, demonstrating immense pace and power down the left flank. He provided the crosses and cut-backs for Aldridge, and was frequently on the scoresheet himself thanks to his fierce shot and expertise with a dead ball. But it was his ability to glide effortlessly past tackles that brought the fans to their feet most often. 'John was a key figure in that side because he could take on three or four defenders, or at least hold the ball long enough to disrupt the opposition's attacking momentum and rhythm,' said Hansen. 'The last Liverpool player who could beat defenders so easily was Steve Heighway in the 1970s – but John was possibly even better.'

VOTE WINNER

Barnes' dazzling form in that first campaign won him the Footballer of the Year and PFA Player of Year accolades. Two years later, after topping the club scoring chart with 28 goals in all competitions, and helping Liverpool secure their 18th League title, he was named Player of the Year for the second time. For many, Barnes was the best footballer in Europe during those first three seasons. However, with English clubs banned from continental action as a result of the Heysel tragedy, he was unable to demonstrate his skills against elite European opponents.

BREAKING DOWN THE BARRIERS

Although players from ethnic backgrounds had started to make their mark on the game before Barnes, he was one of English football's first black superstars. He faced down the racial hostility that was still evident at some grounds, dealing with one particularly unsavoury banana-throwing incident with typical class: when the fruit landed at his feet while he prepared to take a corner, he simply back heeled it off pitch.

For a time, Barnes was unarguably the most skilful player in Britain, possibly even the world. He turned himself into a hero for fans of all colours, and succeeded in making the peddlers of prejudice look outdated and ridiculous. His MBE, awarded in 1990, was as much for his success in breaking down racial barriers as for his services to football.

MIDFIELD REINVENTION

Barnes' ability to sashay past defenders made him a target for the game's hard men, but he managed to remain remarkably injury-free throughout his peak years. He later attributed this to an 'animal instinct', explaining: 'In the jungle, animals sense when a lion prowls nearby.

Humans have similar intuition on the football field. If a really hard tackle came in I took evasive action – I was able to anticipate and react quicker than most players.'

It was while on England duty that he finally did pick up a serious knee injury that deprived him of his searing pace. However, once he recovered, he converted to a deeper midfield role where he continued to shine with his sublime passing. He also proved the ideal role model for a new generation of players like Robbie Fowler and Steve McManaman – with whom he combined brilliantly in the 1995 League Cup final. However, by the end of the following season, it

was time to bring down the curtain on nine glorious seasons at Anfield.

MAN OF MANY PARTS

After leaving Liverpool, Barnes continued his playing career with Charlton and Newcastle. He also tried his hand at coaching, both at Celtic and Tranmere, carved out a new role as a TV sports presenter, and has worked as an ambassador for the charity, Save The Children.

He'll also be forever famous for his contributions to two of football's best-ever pop songs: England's 1990 World Cup anthem 'World In Motion', and Liverpool's own 1988 hit, 'The Anfield Rap'.

OPPOSITE TOP: John Barnes demonstrates the speed and skill that left most defenders trailing

OPPOSITE LEFT: Back of the net: Barnes celebrates one of his 108 Liverpool goals

ABOVE: John Barnes during his debut season at Anfield

Steven Gerrard

STEVIE WONDER

A full list of Steven Gerrard's records and achievements could fill a book on their own, as could the quotes about his footballing skills and leadership qualities. No other player of the last quarter-century comes close to matching his influence and impact on Liverpool FC. For many, he's the finest player to emerge from Britain for a generation. Legendary Real Madrid and France playmaker Zinedine Zidane has described him as 'the most complete midfielder in the world'.

FROM SCHOOLBOY TO STAR

At the age of nine, Gerrard joined Liverpool's Youth Academy where coach Steve Heighway quickly recognised him as a star of the future. 'Outstanding potential has to be recognised and nurtured, and Steven Gerrard, a gem from Huyton, could be next on our production line,' wrote Heighway. 'Our staff are genuinely excited by his prospects'. They were right to be. Gerrard became a senior team regular while still a teenager, and won his first England cap just one day after his 20th birthday. Within a year of that appearance he helped his club win a historic treble of FA, UEFA and League Cup trophies. The 2000–01 season ended with him being voted PFA Young Player of the Year.

CAPTAIN FANTASTIC

From the outset, Gerrard displayed the qualities that were to become his trademarks: endless running, superb passing, strong tackling and ferocious shooting. He inspired his team-mates as well as the Anfield crowd, and it was no surprise when he was handed the captain's armband in October 2003.

Gerrard thrived on the responsibility, displaying bravery and courage, spurring the team on with a never-say-die attitude, and making a habit of scoring vital and, often spectacular, goals. One of his most memorable was against Olympiacos in December 2004 – an incredible

86th minute strike into the Kop net that ensured Liverpool's progress in the Champions League just as they appeared to be on their way out.

Five months later, when defeat in the final against AC Milan seemed certain, his headed goal sparked the extraordinary comeback that ended with the Reds overturning a 0–3 deficit and winning the resulting penalty shoot-out.

THE GERRARD FINAL

Gerrard finished the next season as the club's top scorer with 23 goals, the last of them coming in an astonishing FA Cup final display against West Ham. He equalised twice, the second the result of a blistering 30-yard volley in the dying seconds. Despite struggling through the 30 minutes of extra time with agonising cramp, he then volunteered for the penalty shoot-out, converting his spot-kick to help deliver another improbable victory.

As a result of his momentous performance that day, Gerrard became the only player to score in European Cup, UEFA Cup, League Cup and FA Cup finals. Another legendary goalscorer was there to witness his unique achievement. 'He's an incredible talent and certainly the best Liverpool player of his generation,' said Ian Rush afterwards. 'But if he had been playing for West Ham and not us, I think they would have won the Cup. He was that influential on the match.'

AND THE WINNER IS...

As well as winning a European Cup, two FA Cups, three League Cups, UEFA Cup and a Super Cup, Gerrard has collected a vast array of personal awards including UEFA Club Player of the Year in 2005, Players' Player of the Year in 2006, and Footballer of the Year in 2009. He has been named in the PFA Team of the Year a record seven times, and the FIFA World XI on three occasions. In 2006 he topped an International Federation of Football History & Statistics poll to be named 'World's Most Popular Footballer'.

STEVIE FOR ENGLAND

Gerrard made his 100th international appearance in November 2012, becoming one of only seven players to win more than a century of England caps. He has been selected more times for his country than any other Liverpool player, and has overtaken Emlyn Hughes as the man with most appearances as captain of the national side. As well as competing in two World Cups, he's taken part in three European Championships. At Euro 2012 he was the only Englishman to be named in the UEFA 'Team of the Tournament'.

GREATEST EVER?

With his place in the list of Anfield legends assured, it's fair to ask where Gerrard ranks in the list of all-time greats. Many Reds fans who watched their team during their most successful period cite Graeme Souness as the ultimate midfielder and captain. Alan Hansen, who played alongside his fellow Scot, can testify to his awesome qualities, but he still rates today's skipper ahead of him. 'Gerrard is Souness with pace,' says Hansen, 'and that's one hell of a player.'

OPPOSITE TOP: Penalty-master: Gerard converts a spot-kick at Old Trafford in September 2010

OPPOSITE RIGHT: His finest hour: Steven Gerrard holds the European Cup aloft in Istanbul

LEFT: Determination all over his face, Gerrard tussles with Chelsea's Didier Drogba

Appendix 1: Roll of Honour
Major Honours

Club Facts
Name: Liverpool Football Club
Nickname: The Reds
Established: 1892
Founder: John Houlding
Crest: The Liver Bird
Sponsor: Standard Chartered Bank
Ground: Anfield
Address: Liverpool FC, Anfield Road, Liverpool, L4 OTH
Manager: Brendan Rodgers
Directors: J. Henry (Principal Owner), T. Werner (Chairman),
D. Ginsberg (Vice-Chairman), I. Ayre (Managing Director),
M. Gordon

Previous Managers
1892–96: John McKenna/
W.E. Barclay
1896–1915: Tom Watson
1919–22: David Ashworth
1923–28: Matt McQueen
1928–36: George Patterson
1936–51: George Kay
1951–56: Don Welsh
1956–59: Phil Taylor
1959–74: Bill Shankly
1974–83: Bob Paisley
1983–85: Joe Fagan
1985–91: Kenny Dalglish
1991–94 Graeme Souness
1994–98: Roy Evans
1998: Roy Evans/Gerard Houllier
1998–2004: Gerard Houllier
2004–10: Rafael Benitez
2010–11: Roy Hodgson
2011–12: Kenny Dalglish

League Champions (18)
1900–01, 1905–06, 1921–22,
1922–23, 1946–47, 1963–64,
1965–66, 1972–73, 1975–76,
1976–77, 1978–79, 1979–80,
1981–82, 1982–83, 1983–84,
1985–86, 1987–88, 1989–90
Runners-up (11): 1898–99, 1909–10,
1968–69, 1973–74, 1974–75,
1977–78, 1984–85, 1986–87,
1988–89, 1990–91, 2008–09

European Cup Winners (5)
1976–77, 1977–78, 1980–81,
1983–84, 2004–05
Runners-up (3): 1984–85, 2006–07

FA Cup Winners (7)
1964–65, 1973–74, 1985–86,
1988–89, 1991–92, 2000–01,
2005–06
Runners-up (7): 1913–14, 1949–50,
1970–71, 1976–77, 1987–88,
1995–96, 2011–12

League Cup Winners (8)
1980–81, 1981–82, 1982–83,
1983–84, 1994–95, 2000–01,
2002–03, 2011–2012
Runners-up (3): 1977–78, 1986–87,
2004–05

UEFA Cup Winners (3)
1972–73, 1975–76, 2000–01

European Super Cup Winners (3)
1977, 2001, 2005
Runners-up (2): 1979, 1985

FA Charity Shield Winners (15)
1964*, 1965*, 1966, 1974, 1976,
1977*, 1979, 1980, 1982, 1986*,
1988, 1989, 1990*, 2001, 2006
* shared
Runners-up: 1922, 1971, 1983, 1992,
2002

ABOVE: The comeback kings. Steven Gerrard lifts the European Cup after the Reds' staggering victory over AC Milan in Istanbul in 2005

RIGHT: Treble glory. The Reds' UEFA Cup triumph over Alaves was their third success in the 2000–01 season

Appendix 2: Other Honours

THE FIRST DOUBLE

Liverpool ended their inaugural season as Champions of the Lancashire League. They won 17 matches, drew two and lost three – exactly the same record as rivals Blackpool, who they pipped by virtue of a superior goal average (goals for, divided by goals against).

One week after their league programme finished, they met Everton in the final of the Liverpool Senior Cup. The first-ever Merseyside derby was a bad tempered and controversial affair, played before 10,000 fans at Bootle's Hawthorne Road ground. Liverpool won 1–0 but Everton lodged an immediate appeal, complaining bitterly about 'the general incompetence of the referee'. This was duly dismissed and Liverpool's Cup, along with Lancashire League trophy, subsequently went on display at one of the city's leading jewellers. But, on 1 September 1893, the store was subject to a break-in and both pieces

of silverware were stolen. Liverpool's board had to stump up £130 to buy replacements.

LOYAL JOE

Liverpool's 5–1 victory over Corinthians in the 1906 Dewar Shield – an early forerunner of the Charity Shield – was largely thanks to a hat-trick from Joe Hewitt. The Chester-born forward played for the Reds between 1904 and 1910, then re-joined as a coach 12 months later. He then went on to serve the club in various roles, including steward and press box attendant, for almost 60 years.

PROMOTED AS CHAMPIONS

After their Lancashire League triumph Liverpool were elected to the Football League and entered into Division Two. Amazingly, they went through the whole campaign unbeaten and ended it at the top of the table. They lasted only one season in the top flight before being

relegated. But, in John McKenna's last year as manager, they became Division Two champions again, scoring an incredible 106 goals in 30 League games – still a club record.

The Reds have won the Second Division title twice since then. In 1904–05, when they topped the table only 12 months after dropping down. And in 1961–62 when Bill Shankly led them back to the top flight after eight years in the wilderness. Promotion that year was secured with a 2–0 victory over Southampton, with both goals coming from Kevin Lewis.

SENIOR CITIZENS

The Reds have enjoyed spectacular success in the Liverpool County FA's 'Senior Cup' tournament winning the competition on 40 occasions since 1893. Although the Reserves participated from the mid-sixties onwards, the competition – featuring both professional and amateur sides – was once the preserve of the first

ABOVE: Jay Spearing and his Liverpool team-mates celebrate winning the 2007 FA Youth Cup

team, and a means of maintaining derby matches during Liverpool's Division Two days. Legendary striker Ian St. John has reason to remember the competition with fondness. He made his debut in a Senior Cup final against Everton in May 1961 – and scored a hat-trick.

SCREEN SPORT SUPER CUP
Following the Heysel tragedy, the Football League devised a new tournament for English clubs who were denied entry to European competition because of the UEFA ban. The Super Cup was originally intended to run for as a long as the ban lasted, but was in fact only staged once, spilling over into the 1986–87 season because of fixture congestion.

After winning their group matches against Southampton and Tottenham, the Reds beat Norwich in the semis. They then had to wait another four months before facing Everton in the two-legged final – beating them 3–1 at Anfield, then 4–1 at Goodison Park. Ian Rush finished as the tournament's top scorer with seven goals – five of them against Everton.

STARS OF THE FUTURE
Liverpool's Academy starlets have won the FA Youth Cup on three occasions, beating West Ham, Manchester United and Manchester City to lift the trophy. The competition has served as a springboard for some of England's top players, and never more so than in 1996, when Liverpool's Jamie Carragher and Michael Owen lined up against West Ham's Rio Ferdinand and Frank Lampard.

OTHER HONOURS
Lancashire League (1)
1892–93

Division Two Champions (4)
1893–94, 1895–96, 1904–05, 1961–62

Sheriff of London Charity Shield/ Dewar Shield (1)
1906

Lancashire Senior Cup (11)
1919, 1920 (shared), 1924, 1931, 1933, 1944, 1947, 1956, 1959, 1973, 2010

Liverpool Senior Cup (40)
1893, 1901, 1902, 1903, 1905, 1907, 1909, 1910 (shared), 1912 (shared), 1913, 1915, 1920, 1925, 1927, 1929, 1930, 1934 (shared), 1936 (shared), 1937, 1939, 1942, 1943, 1946, 1947, 1948, 1951, 1952, 1962, 1964 (shared), 1968, 1977, 1980, 1981, 1982 (shared), 1997, 1998, 2002, 2004, 2009, 2010

Screen Sport Super Cup (1)
1987

Central League (Reserves) (16)
1956–57, 1968–69, 1969–70, 1970–71, 1972–73, 1973–74, 1974–75, 1975–76, 1976–77, 1978–79, 1979–80, 1980–81, 1981–82, 1983–84, 1984–85, 1989–90

Premier Reserve League North (2)
1999–2000, 2007–08

Premier Reserve League National Champions (1)
2007–08

FA Youth Cup (3)
1996, 2006, 2007

ABOVE: Liverpool team photograph on becoming champions of Division Two in 1961–62

ABOVE: Liverpool Youth Team manager Gary Ablett at Anfield with the Premier League Youth Team Cup 2007–08

Index

Page numbers in *italic* type refer to pictures; **bold** numbers refer to main profiles.

Picture Credits

The publishers would like to thank the following sources for their kind permission to reproduce the pictures in this book.

Imagery © Liverpool Football Club & Athletic Grounds Ltd. with the following exceptions:

Colorsport: 21B, 33, 36, 38TL, 44L, 82TR, 86BL, 111B, 130BR, 131, 139; /Andrew Cowie: 49BL, 92TL

Getty Images: 38BR, 90TL; /Gunnar Berning/Bongarts: 86BC; /Shaun Botterill: 106B; /Simon Bruty: 125T; /David Cannon: 93BR, 118L; /Central Press: 88BL; /Mike Clarke/AFP: 94R; /Phil Cole: 40TL, 65TR; /Paul Ellis/AFP: 27TR; /Luke Eppel/WireImage: 42; /Stu Forster: 28B, 91TL; /Laurence Griffiths:

37, 47, 68BR; /Richard Heathcote: 57TR; /Hulton Archive: 133BR; /Karim Jaafar/AFP: 92BR; /Alex Livesey: 26BR, 143; /Clive Mason: 26TL; /Jamie McDonald: 98TR; /Jonathan Nackstrand/AFP: 88T; /John Peters: 154BL; /Popperfoto: 130T; /Gary M Prior: 65B; /Ben Radford: 79TR, 89TL, 101BL, 103TR, 148BL; /Michael Regan: 117; /Clive Rose: 22-23; /Martin Rose/Bongarts: 81TR; /Jewel Samad/AFP: 86L; /Robert Stiggins/Express: 85TL; /Bob Thomas: 13BR, 16B, 27B, 32, 50B, 54BL, 66T, 113T, 124B, 140BL; /Bob Thomas/Popperfoto: 15B, 103BL, 122T; /Mark Thompson: 71BL; /Andrew Yates/AFP: 29TR

Mirrorpix: 126BL

Offside Sports Photography: /Gerry Cranham: 87; /Mirrorpix: 49TR, 141

Press Association Images: 19, 123R, 142BL; /Bernat Armangue/AP: 87BL; /Peter Byrne: 85B; /Mike Egerton: 76TR; /Tom Hevezi: 41TL; /Dominic Lipinski: 121B; /Dave Munden: 13TL; /Phil O'Brien: 46; /David Rawcliffe: 107B; /Martin Rickett: 44BR, 94BR; /Peter Robinson: 101TR, 119T, 120; /William Stevens/AP: 147TR